The Resilient Mind

The
Resilient
Mind

Conquer Your Fears,
Channel Your Anxiety,
and Bounce Back Stronger

Dr. John Demartini

Published 2023 by Gildan Media LLC
aka G&D Media
www.GandDmedia.com

Front cover design by David Rheinhardt of Pyrographx

Interior design by Meghan Day Healey of Story Horse, LLC

Library of Congress Cataloging-in-Publication Data is available upon request

ISBN: 978-1-7225-0618-6

10   9   8   7   6   5   4   3   2   1

Contents

Contents

Resilience Is a Sign of Wisdom

How well and quickly do you recover from difficult, tough, or challenging events?

How quickly do you bounce back from circumstances that try you?

How elastic, flexible, or pliable are you when you are being tested almost to the limit?

Does your life demonstrate masterful plasticity when faced with adversity?

Do you have true grit and resolve?

Do you rise from the ashes after facing challenges or traumas?

If you feel unable to adapt to a constantly changing world, your distress levels are likely to increase and you are more likely to be button pushed and distracted by perceptions of loss of what you seek and gain of what you avoid.

Endurance and resilience are essential for a well-lived life. Your ability to absorb shocking news with equanimity is a sign of maturity, wisdom, and mastery. The fortitude and courage to remain poised, or return to poise after being challenged, regardless of perceived circumstances, is essential for living an exemplary, leadership-positioned life.

It is not so much what happens to you that truly matters as much as your responses—your perceptions, decisions, and actions. They give you power. Furthermore, you have control over them. Taking command of these neurologically driven processes can make the difference between being a victim of your history and being a master of your destiny.

Two primary areas in your brain affect the way you act or react to stimuli and events. One is the amygdala, a subcortical area, sometimes called "the desire center," which comes online when you are in survival mode and are emotionally (sometimes foolishly) overreacting to life. Its response is sometimes called "systems 1 thinking," because it is fast reacting and is designed for perceptions of emergency, as subjectively perceived. It reacts before it thinks. It is the seat of hindsight. The amygdala is particularly responsible for impulses, instincts, and short-term gratification. It is reflexive more than reflective and narrow-minded more than broad-minded.

Because this desire center is more subjective and biased, it is generally more polarized emotionally and is often associated with rigid absolutes. It fires off when you are seeking prey (goal supportive opportunities) and avoiding predator (goal challenging threats). It assigns emotional valency or charge and initiates elevated dopamine and/or adrenaline responses. It speeds up the aging process and can curtail your immunity. Aging is a symptom of non-resilience. In fact, all emotions are symptoms of non-resilience, because they're violent; they're not neutral.

The second area is the prefrontal cortex, sometimes called "the executive function center," which comes online when you are in "thrival" mode, thoughtfully and wisely proacting in life. It is sometimes called "systems 2 thinking" because it is slower acting than the amygdala. It is designed for more balanced perceptions, thoughtful decisions, actions of utility, meaningful and objective strategies, and longer-term purposeful pursuits. It is the seat of foresight and reflection. It thinks before it reacts. The prefrontal cortex is more responsible for inspired long-term vision, strategic planning, mitigating risks, executing plans, and self-governance.

Because the executive center is more objective, it is more neutral and adaptable and less prone to fear of loss or gain. It balances out your neurochemistry, governing and enhancing your autonomic and immune functions. Its resultant alpha and gamma waves synchronize the rest of the brain with the heart. In this area, a greater level of patience, poise, and resilience is born.

So how do you awaken your executive center?

This is where living according to your highest priorities comes into play.

You have a unique, specific set of values or priorities by which you live your daily life: your hierarchy of values. You are spontaneously and intrinsically inspired to do and fulfill whatever is highest on your list of values. This is where you are most disciplined, reliable, and focused. Because these areas are most important and valuable to you, you require no extrinsic motivation to act here. You spontaneously pursue these highest-priority items.

When you fill your day with high-priority actions, your blood, glucose, and oxygen flow into your executive center, and you become more strategic, objective, and resilient. You wake up the natural-born leader that may be lying dormant within, and your life is less likely to fill up with distressful challenges.

But when you do not take command of your day and live according to your highest priorities, lower-priority distractions will inevitably emerge and possibly engulf you. You will become more vulnerable to outside opportunists and time-consuming distractors. Your blood glucose and oxygen will begin to flow down more into the amygdala, initiating a series of reactive, rigid, subjectively biased, and ungoverned survival reactions. The amygdala and the corresponding impulses and instincts of the gut brain will begin dominating your behavior, and generating less efficient and effective distress responses. The hypothalamus and pituitary will stimulate your adrenal glands, which will pump out cortisol, and the distress response will shrink your space and time horizons and initiate immediately gratifying survival reactions. Now you will react before you think. You will have to learn through hindsight and trial and error instead of foresight and thoughtful strategic planning. You are now less effective at perceiving, deciding, and acting. You have become vulnerable to outer circumstances instead of pursuing the inner yearnings and the inspirations of your heart.

Ultimately, it is how well you live according to your priorities that will determine your level of resilience.

When you have "knocked your day out of the ball-park," as some say, through living with a clearly priori-tized agenda and checking off the highest-priority actions, you feel on top of the world. You go through your day and come home with more resilience to face whatever is wait-ing for you.

When you let your perceptions of the outer world's challenges dictate your reactions and you deal with low-priority distractions all day, you can become a grizzly bear—ready to overreact—both throughout your day and upon returning home.

The material in this book will give you many more details about your brain, how it works, and how you can use its functioning to create your optimal life. You'll learn how to determine your own hierarchy of values and how to put it into practice in order to create an empowered, creatively fulfilled, and more resilient life.

You, your coworkers, and your loved ones deserve you as your most authentic self, ready with resilience to inspire, lead, and exemplify. So prioritize your daily actions, del-egating your lower priorities to those who would love to take them away. Say yes to what is most important and meaningful and no to all the rest. Give yourself permission to master your life with resilience and live with wisdom.

This book will show you how. Here are a few of things you'll learn:

- How to determine your individual hierarchy of values
- How to adopt the power of living in accordance with your highest value
- How to change your brain functioning to enhance your level of resilience
- How to overcome depression—without medication
- How to handle anxiety
- How to move past grief over the perceptions of lost loved ones

Chapter 1
Your Hierarchy of Values

Resilience is a natural by-product of living by priority. To understand what I mean by this, let's look at the hierarchy of your values.

Every human being has a unique hierarchy of values: things that are most important, second most important, third most important, and so on. You spontaneously focus on the things that are highest on your value system; you seldom if ever get around to doing things that are lower on your list of values. Have you ever noticed that you find or make the time to do the things that are most important to you, but you don't seem to get around to doing the things that are not as important?

I don't believe that procrastination really exists. When somebody looks at another individual and says, "God, they procrastinate a lot!" they're projecting their own values onto them. The other individual is living according to their own value system. You may label them as lazy procrastinators, but in reality they're doing what's important to them at that moment. They just may not be doing what's important to you. Each individual tends to spontaneously do what is most important to them instead of what is less important to them, though it may be most important to you. When you label them as procrastinators, it generally means you are projecting your higher values onto them and expecting them to live in your higher values and not their own, which is a lesson in futility.

Our misunderstanding sometimes leads us to mislabel people, but in fact everybody lives moment by moment according to their own hierarchy of values—they make decisions according to what they believe will provide them with the greatest advantage in that moment. The hierarchy of their values dictates their destiny. The hierarchy of your values dictates *your* destiny. Some of those values are changing; others are more stable and steady. You might call them core values or more lasting values: values that guide your life for a long period of time.

Your values dictate how you perceive the world. Let me use an analogy here. Say you have a husband and wife with three young children. The husband is working extra hours, and the wife is staying home and raising the family. Her highest value is her children, their education, their health, and the home. The husband's mission is to work and provide economic support.

Say this couple is walking through a shopping mall. The wife is filtering her perceptions of that mall according to her value system. She notices toys, children's outfits—anything that would help those children. Out of the whole environment, she's selectively attending to those things. The husband, on the other hand, is noticing *Forbes* magazine, computers, and other things that might assist him in business. Each is filtering out the world around them according to their own hierarchy of values. She will probably not even notice business opportunities, and he probably won't even notice children's clothes.

Neither of them is right or wrong; they're just unique. The uniqueness of our lives is expressed according to our hierarchy of values. Nobody really has right or wrong values, except to somebody who has a similar or different set of values. I've been blessed to interact with thousands of people and observe their value systems, and I've yet to see one that's exactly the same as another. We may be the same in our spiritual essence, but our outer more existential form is unique, and so are our sets of values.

Attention and Video Games

The hierarchy of values affects the way we sense the world in another respect. You've heard of attention deficit disorder. Every child that's labeled with "attention deficit disorder" also has an "attention surplus order" to balance it. For every attention deficit disorder, there's an attention surplus order.

What does that mean? It means that the child can sit there and focus on a video game for nine hours straight, without distraction; they'll know every single character or individual, every move, and every action in that game, and they'll sometimes even have a photographic memory of it.

Do they really have an attention deficit disorder in what they value most? No, they have a heightened attention and concentration. They have a unique hierarchy of values.

The teacher who's frustrated and unsuccessfully attempting to teach the child may not have learned the art of communicating in terms of the child's highest values. Sometimes they label the child because they themselves haven't mastered this more respectful form of communicating in terms of the child's hierarchy of values. The second they do, the child awakens to that information.

I was in Brisbane, Australia, twenty years ago, and I had a mother whose sixteen-year-old son had his head into video games and computers. She was a single mom, she was working hard, and she felt that it was time that her son was to go out and get a job. She was living in a different era mentally and was expecting him to do a paper route or something like that. The son didn't live in that world, so she hired me to consult with him and get him back on track.

I went into his room and said, "So your mom's on your case, huh?"

"Yeah."

"What are you working on?"

"I'm working on creating a video game."

"That sounds amazing. Are you pretty skilled at it?"

"Yeah."

"Do you love doing that?"

"I love playing video games, and I also love designing software for such games."

"Do you know how to do it really well?"

"Yeah."

"So you are great at it?"

"Yeah."

"Would you be willing to show me what you're up to and working on."

He showed me what he could do. I said, "This is quite ingenious. You're very adept at this."

"I know. My mom doesn't understand it. She doesn't even know how to turn on a computer. I guess that's why her repressions are my expressions, as I heard you state at your recent talk." (In case you didn't know, the children will sometimes specialize in whatever the parents have repressed.)

When I came out of that room, the mother asked, "Did you talk some sense into him?"

"No, I hired him." Today he's almost thirty-six years old and has already worked for companies like IBM for a quarter of a million dollars a year.

Autocratic behavior is not the way to get what you would love from your children. It's finding out what inspires them and caring enough about them and understanding and respecting their values. That way, you can communicate what you would love for them to do in a way that makes sense to them and fulfills their highest values.

If your child is required to take certain classes or attend certain social events, communicate the value for these objectives in terms of his or her highest values and they will become more engaged. Nobody is spontaneously inspired to go to a class unless they perceive it to be fulfilling their highest values. The second they see how it is, they yearn to learn and excel. If not, they're not engaged, and they just want to get out and escape the unfulfilling so-called educational experience.

The key is to care enough about your children to communicate that way. I presented a class in the township of Alexandria, South Africa, an economically impoverished area. It started with a high school pass rate of 27 percent. In one year, we took it to a 97 percent pass rate. The metric changed when we showed them how the classes would help them fulfill what they valued most individually. I helped them determine their highest values, and I also helped determine the teachers' highest values. Then I helped them link the classes to the teachers' highest values and to the students' highest values. Then I linked the students' highest values to the teachers', and vice versa, to enhance communication and respect. The pass rate went from 27 to 97 percent, because students spontaneously want to learn what is most meaningful and important to them, but if they can't see how what they are being told to learn is helping them fulfill what they value most, they're turned off.

As parents and teachers, we are wise to respect the children and their highest values instead of autocratically forcing them to go against what they value most. If we don't, they'll succeed in terms of short-term memory at best: they'll pass the test, but they won't really be inspired to learn. I believe there's a genius in every child, and I've watched it come out once you know how to engage them and respectfully manage their higher value-driven learning experience.

Our hierarchy of values dictates how we perceive and act upon the world. Areas that are high on our list of values tend to become more ordered and organized. We tend to be undisciplined, unfocused, and chaotic in regard to things of low value. In other words, the higher the value, the more the order; the lower the value, the more chaos.

Nothing really distracts you from what's at the peak of your value system. You'll sacrifice anything lower for it. A mother who has her child as her highest value will leave work if something happens to the child. If her highest value is making income, she'll go to work even if the child is sick, because work is most important to her. It's not that the children are unimportant; it's that the woman's hierarchy of values dictates how she will act or react. Again, nobody's right or wrong for attempting to do what is most important, meaningful, and fulfilling according to their own unique set of highest values.

Whenever we perceive that we are able to fulfill whatever is highest on our list of values we become more empowered, adaptable, and resilient. The same for our children.

Marriage: Complementary Opposites

If you have something that's high on your value list, you can commonly marry somebody who has it lower on theirs, so you have complementary opposites that stabilize the relationship dynamic. The purpose of marriage is not to find somebody exactly like yourself, but to find somebody who represents your disowned parts, so they can love and fulfill that part of you that you assume to be missing in order to help make you feel more whole. In actuality, nothing is missing in either you or them; it just appears to be. And it is such apparent voids that drive your and their hierarchy of values.

If you've gotten married for the sake of a one-sided hedonic happiness, just know that's an illusion. The purpose of marriage is not hedonic happiness; it's to bring to wholeness the parts we're disowning so as to attain fulfillment, meaning, and purpose.

Your purpose is an expression of mostly your highest value and partly your second and third highest values. Nobody has to motivate you to do the things that are highest on your value list. In my view, there's a difference between inspiration and motivation. Inspiration is when you are aligned and attuned to your highest values; you know yourself, and you're spontaneously acting accordingly. Motivation is trying to be something else, so only outside influence or incentives will keep you at what you're doing.

Your mission in life is attuning to and living according to your highest values. You can learn what they are from a variety of value determinants: the way you fill your intimate and personal space most; the way you spend your time and money most; what energizes you most; what dominates your thinking, visualizing, and internal dialoguing about how you would love your life to be that shows evidence of coming true most; what you converse with other people about most; what inspires you most; your most persistent goals that are coming true; and what you spontaneously love to learn about most.

If you go to my office, you'll see books, so obviously one of my higher values is studying and learning the laws of the universe as they relate to human behavior and the evolution of consciousness. Nobody has to motivate me to do that, because it's intrinsically important to me. But somebody might find it expedient to motivate me to do something that's low on my value list—like cooking or driving.

Again when we are fulfilling what is most important to us, we become most resilient.

Wisdom in life is learning how to delegate things that are lower on your list of values, and to know what things are higher on your value list and stick to them. Then you can link things of lower value to those that are higher value, so items of less importance can become more inspiring for you to do until you can delegate them. For instance: *How specifically will doing this particular lower value action, duty, or responsibility—temporarily, until I can fully delegate it— help me fulfill what is currently highest on my list of values, my mission or purpose?*

Wisdom is paying close attention to the people you love and identifying how they fill their space, how they spend their energy, time, and money, their conversation, and what they love learning. To the degree that you can know their highest values and honor and communicate in terms of them is the degree to which you will have respectful and fulfilling relationships.

When your actions align fully with your highest values, you feel more inspired, you love what you do, and you're doing what you love.

There was a story about a woman who stepped out of her house and saw three wise men with long white beards outside.

"Who are you?" the woman asked.

One man spoke up. "This gentleman over here is Wealth. This gentleman over here is Success, and I'm Love. Is your husband home?"

The woman went in and told her husband that there were three wise men outside. He said, "Why don't you invite them in?"

She went out to invite them in, but they said, "No, we can only go in one at a time, so choose which one of us you'd like to come in."

The woman went back and asked her husband, "Which one shall I let in?"

"Bring in Wealth," he said.

"No, I think I'd like to bring in Success."

The daughter, who was there, said, "No, bring in Love; we need more love in the family."

The woman said, "Maybe you're right; bring in Love." She went out and said, "We'd like to have you come in first, Mr. Love."

Love got up and walked in, and the other two started to follow.

The woman said, "I thought that only one of you could come in at a time."

"No, if you'd asked for Success, he would have walked in. If you'd asked for Wealth, he would have walked in. But since you asked for Love, all three of us walk in, because wherever love goes, so do success and wealth."

In other words, when we find out what's in our heart and follow what's highest on our values list, we are moving toward alignment with what is most inspiring, meaningful, and fulfilling in our individual universe. We naturally draw in the most resonant people, places, things, and events that help us fulfill our life.

Many people go through life wandering around and seldom paying attention to themselves. But as the Delphic Oracle in ancient Greece said, "Know thyself." To the degree that we know our highest values, we understand why we react and why we label things as we do. We also know what our mission is, because our mission is an expression and fulfillment of our highest values.

When we are fulfilling our mission, we become most resilient and adaptable to whatever happens in our world.

Moments of Inspiration

One sign that we're on track with our highest values is that we have moments of inspiration. Have you ever watched a movie or listened to a piece of music and got tears of inspiration in your eyes? At that moment, it is wise to identify and write out exactly what is going on as well as the words or lyrics that inspired you. In those moments, those lyrics have a special meaning for you.

I went back in my life, scanned through the music that inspired me, even when I was a teenager, and bought the tapes or CDs. I listened to that music again, and right when I got the same tear of inspiration, I wrote down the lyrics. I compiled those lyrics and found out that they were the primary message that I share today in my seminars.

Tears of inspiration come at moments when you're most authentic, in tune with your highest value(s). Your physiology and psychology are giving you feedback to let you know you're on track; you're present; you're inspired; you're authentic. Every time you have that experience, identify it. Identify the words that inspired you and find out exactly what's going through your mind at that time. Then structure your life around their essence and watch how more adaptable, empowered, and resilient you become.

The Love List

To express your mission in life, it's helpful to write down what you know you love. I call it a love list. It's not an infatuation list; that's some fantasy that's not doable or achievable. It's something that you know in your heart you'd love to do; it may have been with you for many years. Start from what you know, and work your way out into what you don't know. That way, what you know grows, and what you don't know is consumed by what you know. Keep writing, rereading, and refining.

I started doing this when I was seventeen. At that point, I had the opportunity to meet a great teacher who helped me identify what I would love to do for the rest of my life. Today I'm doing it. After a few edits what I then wrote became: *I dedicate my life to the study of universal laws as they relate to body, mind, and soul, and particularly to healing. I want to travel the world and share my inspiration, to be a teacher, healer, and philosopher.* I wrote those things down and read them over thousands of times. I visualized them, affirmed them, and kept focusing on and refining them.

To unfold your mission, start with what you know and let what you know grow and keep refining it. At first, it's possibly a little unclear and volatile, but eventually it becomes stable. Say to yourself, "I am now unveiling my magnificent and most inspiring and meaningful mission of service to the world."

Many people live in insignificance instead of magnificence. Magnificence comes when we attune to our highest values and allow our most authentic state of being to guide and direct us with tears of inspiration and moments of glimmering wisdom.

If you don't define what you would love to do in your life, somebody else will define it for you. By defining it exactly the way you would love your life to be, you're less likely to have somebody else do that for you.

Your taking command of and designing your life adds to your level of clarity and resilience.

When I was about four years old, I had the job of pulling out weeds from around the house. By the time I finished, I'd be starting over, because it was nutgrass: it drives you nuts. I would pull nutgrass up on one side of the house, and soon it would be back again.

There was a lovely lady who lived next door to us named Mrs. Grubbs. She was a little eighty-something-year-old woman who had flowers and hummingbirds in her beautiful backyard garden. One day, Mrs. Grubbs leaned across the fence and said, "John, if you don't plant flowers, you're going to forever pull weeds."

We had a bag of lima beans in the garage, so I planted beans every four inches around the whole house. My parents were very patient, but after a while, the whole house was surrounded by beanstalks. They knew I meant well, but it was probably disheartening to them to see beans all around the house, which of course they had to eat.

If we don't plant flowers in our garden of our mind, we're going to be pulling weeds forever. Let's decide, "I'm worth it; I'm magnificent. I deserve the time and the effort to masterfully gain insight into my mission. I'm observing my values, my inspiration, what I'd love to do, and I'm focusing on those priority pursuits."

The next step to take to help this mission emerge is to look back at everything that you did as a service or in a career and find the common threads that underlie them. If you make a list of every career you've ever been involved in, you'll find some common unifying elements. The quality of our lives is based on the quality of the questions we ask. If we ask questions that probe deeply into the common threads that are linked to our heart, our heart will reveal our mission.

When identifying our mission, it's valuable to write down all the people that we've perceived as heroes—people about whom we've said, "I'd love to be able to do that or meet that individual." I'm sure you have people that you would have loved to meet. Make a list of them. Again, you'll find there are common threads to those heroes. What you admire in others lies within you, and it is waiting to be recognized and acknowledged.

I love reading the biographies of great people—anybody who's left an immortal effect on history, whether it be in prose, poetry, science, philosophy, or any other field. I love reading the biographies of these individuals, because I think and believe, "If they can do it, so can I." I also look at people who triumphed over the odds. I love to read about them, because it gives me new insights and inspires me to overcome my own perceived challenges. I look for where I too have done the same behaviors to the same degree in my own form. I own the traits that I admire in others and therefore become more reflective in my awareness. I remind myself that "nothing is missing within me. It is just in my own unique form." Many of these people were ridiculed and sometimes violently opposed, and that gives me encouragement too. As Emerson said, "To be great is to be misunderstood." (That's helped me, because I'm not always easily understood.)

Another useful practice is to read your love list every day while saying to yourself, "I am on a mission that is inspiring and magnificent. I have something meaningful, powerful, and incredibly significant to do on this planet." If you believe you are here to do something significant, that's what will come out of your life. If you think small, you'll manifest small. If you think larger, you'll manifest larger. So begin clarifying and defining what that something magnificent is and start taking action and resiliently shining.

Yearning for Immortality

At the end of your life, you will not like to think, "Nobody knew who I was; nobody knew I had an impact." You have inside you a yearning for contribution and immortality.

We have an irrational and rational desire in our physical body to live as long as possible and possibly immortally. Most people believe in some form of an information conservation in the afterlife, so there's a part of us that yearns for an immortal expression. Spiritually, we have a desire to live an immortal life. Mentally, we have a desire to leave some contribution of ideas to others that lasts beyond our physical lives. We would like to have our career outlive our life. We don't want it to disappear. We would like to pass it on to our children or to somebody who is working for us; we have a desire to keep that business alive. Financially, most people would like to have more money at the end of their life than life at the end of their money.

There's also a desire to have offspring that will live beyond you. I was jogging with my grandmother, who is in her late nineties. (It was slow, but she was out there.) I asked, "What's the biggest challenge you've faced in your nineties?"

"My children dying before I do." Because that's what was happening: some of her children were dying before she did. Part of her yearned for an immortal expression, to have her children outlive her.

The next goal is to have an impact on society so that you are remembered; you're not just forgotten. And of course, physically, we want to have our bodies live as long as we want. We have a magnificent yearning for an immortal expression.

How do we make such an immortal impact? First, we clarify our highest value-based mission. Concentrating on our mission could be likened to concentrating light through a magnifying glass: we bring enthusiasm to our lives and come on fire. If you're enthused, you magnetize and draw more people than if you're uninspired and a dud. People who are certain, empowered, and enthusiastic and are inspired by what they do draw opportunities to themselves and leave a more immortal impact directly or through the ripple effect.

A Big Enough Why

To make a difference in the world, you will require a big enough *why*. At a recent seminar of mine, a gentleman said, "I really would love to do this."

"How long have you been loving to do that?"

"Oh, for about ten years."

"And you haven't done it?"

"No."

"Then," I said, "it's not really something you'd love to do."

"What do you mean?"

"If you really loved to do it, you'd do it. So you're probably trying to live somebody else's life."

When you get a big enough *why*, the *hows* will take care of themselves. If you don't have a big enough why, the hows won't take care of themselves.

Alfred Marshall, who wrote a book called *Principles of Economics*, said that any degree of human motive can be measured economically. We can find out exactly what drives you and how much it would cost to buy or initiate a particular action or stop that action.

Let's say you smoke, and I offered you $2,000 not to smoke for the next ten minutes. You'd say, "I can handle it for ten minutes." If I gave you $20,000, could you do it for an hour?

If you're not manifesting your dream and you're procrastinating, this means the required action steps to achieve the dream are lower on your value list than something else. What if I said, "I'm going to give you $1 million if you get that done in the next forty-eight hours"? Would you get it done? The cash incentive association would temporarily place it high on your value list. The point is, if I give you a big enough *why* to initiate the required actions, you'll do it. When the why is big enough, the hows take care of themselves.

When you can link whatever you say you would love to do to your highest values, you increase the probability of doing it. If you do, you're going to be more inspired in your life, more resilient, and you're going to have a bigger outreach.

Let me explain why. The more we listen to our most authentic, highest value self, sometimes termed our heart and soul, the more inspired we become. The more inspired we become, the broader our vision. Fear and guilt contract us; love and gratitude expand us. They bring inspiration from the heart. Gratitude is the key that opens up the gateway to the heart, where love and inspiration emerge. It expands our consciousness spontaneously, and we see greater space and time horizons and become more resilient to whatever frightens or distracts us.

We cannot make a difference in ourselves unless we have a cause greater than ourselves. Otherwise our habits will rule us. If you would love to make a difference in yourself, it is essential to have a cause or mission greater than you. If I'm standing up lecturing and I'm worried about what you think of me, I'm thinking about me, so I can't deliver to you. But if I think about you, I don't notice me. I might even have my collar twisted or my zipper undone, but if I'm thinking about you, that doesn't matter. It doesn't throw me off.

As a result, if I want to make a difference in my family, it is essential that I awaken a cause at least as big as my community. If I want to make a difference in my community, I will require a cause as big as my city. If I want to make a difference in my city, I will require a cause as big as my state. If I want to be number one in the state, I will require a national mission and vision, a national cause. If I want to have national impact, I will require a global vision, a global cause. And if I want to leave a global impact on this planet, I will require an astronomical cause. The Greeks laughed at Socrates and Plato for teaching young people astronomy, but they were trying to accustom them to thinking celestially and looking back terrestrially.

As is said, we are spiritual and celestial beings having a physical and terrestrial experience rather than physical beings having a spiritual experience. Yet we tend to think of our lives in terrestrial more than celestial terms. When we sit here and look out, we're overwhelmed by the immensity. When we expand our awareness and influence and step up and out there and look in, the world is ours to build and create. So, if we want to make a major impact on the world, we would be wise to awaken to an astronomical vision.

In his essay "Circles," Emerson says that our authentic self or soul continuously draws us to ever greater concentric spheres, ever greater horizons of space and time in our thinking. I often say that the magnitude of the space and time horizons within our innermost dominant thought determines our level of our conscious evolution. If we think in terms of a bum on the street, who lives day to day, we have a small, contracted evolution. If we think in terms of week to week or month to month, we're still somewhat circumscribed. The magnitude of space and time in our minds is determined by our willingness to listen to our most authentic inspirations. The more we attempt to live in somebody else's higher values and allow the resultant philias and phobias—or feelings of shame and pride—to run our lives, the more we contract ourselves. The sage who is authentic, and more expanded and inspired, thinks in terms of eternity.

If we want to live our mission and make a difference, it's wise to turn inward and discover, expand, and inspire ourselves. We can link the actions we'd love to do to the top values that are most important to us. We will not procrastinate doing things that are inspiring to us. We'll only procrastinate on things that are lower on our value list.

You can also take your love list—the list of objectives you would love to bring into reality—and keep expanding and refining it. I started my love list in 1972. It's now a thirty-three-volume series of books; it's got my dreams as well as my mission statement. I read this on my computer or in hard copy every day. I've learned that if I put my hand into the pot of glue, the glue sticks. If I put my mind into the great works of immortals, and add their ideas to my love list, some of those ideas stick. If I put my mind repeatedly into the great writing moments of my own inspirations, those inspirations start manifesting in my life.

We're here as co-fashioners. We're here to take the matter of this world and mold it according to our most inspired certainty and presence of expression. Whoever has the most powerful expression and concentrated focus will draw the resources from the world around and manifest.

The individual who listens to their innermost authentic self or soul expands their horizon and looks from that greater horizon inward. If you read your mission every day and keep refining it, you will see clearly, and the details you put into it will dissolve the obstructions and challenges you might face, because each detail you leave out can become a challenge that you bring in.

Your innermost dominant thought becomes your outermost tangible reality.

The greater the clarity of your vision, the more resilient your life becomes.

Getting a Gasp of Air

A young man once came up to Socrates saying, "Socrates, I want to be a wise man. I want to learn everything that you have. I want to be and know everything that you know."

Socrates walks the young man up to the beach and takes him into the sea. Finally, Socrates says, "So you want to learn?"

"I want to learn everything; I'm dedicated," says the young man. "I'll be your greatest student."

Socrates jams the young man's head down in the water and holds him there. He starts squirming and fighting a little bit. Then Socrates brings him up. The young man says, "Socrates, I'm serious: I want to learn from you."

"So, you want to learn?" Socrates puts the young man's head down in the water again, and this time holds him down for a minute or two until he is kicking and fighting for his life.

Finally, the young man comes up and says, "Socrates, what the hell are you doing? You're mad. I want to learn from you. It looks like you're trying to kill me."

Socrates holds the young man's head down again and keeps him there for two or three minutes until he goes limp. Then he picks the young man up, takes him onto the beach, lays him out, and revives him. As the young man comes to, spitting out water, Socrates says, "When you want to learn from me as much as you just wanted to get a gasp of air, I'm here to teach you."

When you have a big enough why, which is linked to your highest values, the teacher appears. Guidance, creativity, and everything else that is needed emerges and manifests.

Empowerment and Disempowerment

Now think about this. If somebody comes up to you and highly criticizes you, and then you try to go to work, you're possibly distracted, aren't you? Anyone that you are infatuated with, or anyone that you resent, consumes your mind; they run you, and you're disempowered through the distraction. If you allow yourself to become infatuated or resentful, you allow those individuals to distract and over-power you, and you're then not running your life from within; your imbalanced perceptions of them are now running you. Automatically disempowered, you become emotional, uncertain, and distracted by fantasy or fright.

If you put somebody up on a pedestal, you minimize yourself relative to them. If you put them down and reject them, you're afraid of them coming back up, so again they're distracting. You disempower yourself any time you put yourself above or below somebody, or put them above or below you. When you put somebody above or below you, your misperceptions of them run you. Those you put on a pedestal will eventually end up in the pit, and those you put in the pit you'll eventually put on a pedestal. But the second you equilibrate them and bring them into balance in your own perceptions, you bring them into your heart. Because you care about them, you don't exaggerate or minimize; you don't put them on a pedestal or in a pit. The reality is, they're all worthy of love, but none of us is worthy of being put either in a pit or on a pedestal.

We empower ourselves to the degree that we express that balanced perspective. We disempower ourselves to the degree that we judge and put others on pedestals or in pits. If we want to empower ourselves to live our mission and make an impact in the world, and be resilient, we are wise to master the art of not letting our misperceptions of others around us run us; we are to work at maintaining a balanced perspective. If you can ask quality questions, which bring balance to your perspective, the individuals around you won't run you; *you* will run you. And whoever has the most balanced perspective and loves the most is the one who rules the game.

The Two Sides of Love

If you're in a relationship, sometimes you're attracted to the other individual; at other times, you're repelled. You like them; you dislike them. Attraction, repulsion. "Come close to me"; "Get out of my sight." "Don't leave me"; "Leave me alone." "I want you, baby"; "Stay back and away." We go back and forth in this dynamic, and this is called the dynamics of conditional love. Attraction and repulsion are the two sides of conditional love. At times, you will put the individual you love up on a pedestal; other times, you'll put them down. You support them one time and challenge them the next. You like them, and then you dislike them; you go back and forth.

Relationships will oscillate in this way unless you have a perfectly balanced perspective and you're poised in the presence and grace of a moment of unconditional love. In that moment, you have a sacred intimacy that is indestructible. The rest of it is emotional inner illusions run by perceptions of outer illusions. The individual who's empowered, present, and certain can apperceive* with balance. If

---

* Apperceive: To perceive consciously, with full awareness.

you have imbalance, you have perceptual garbage, and if you put garbage in, you get garbage out.

Our relationships with ourselves and the people around us are distressful to the degree that we have these imbalances of perception. Our relationships are poised, present, and "eustressful" (stressful in a meaningful and wellness producing way) to the degree that we have them synchronously balanced. This is how we empower ourselves. We also empower ourselves by identifying other people's values and caring enough about them to communicate our highest values in terms of theirs.

There is something called *carefulness*, which means minimizing your values and emphasizing the other individual's. You walk on eggshells trying to please them. There's also *carelessness*, where you self-righteously think your higher values are more important, you project your values onto the other individual, and they're "supposed to" live by them.

Then there's *caring*, where you communicate your highest values respectfully in terms of theirs. You honor both equally. This is the key to a fair, sustainable exchange in your relationship that can help it last. It creates resilience, poise, and endurance. The others are oscillating, temporary emotional states.

If you put somebody on a pedestal, you submit to their values system. When you hear yourself saying, "I should be doing this," or "I'm supposed to be doing that," you're injecting their values into your life. You're minimizing yourself relative to some outer authority, and you're giving that authority and its value system the authorship and governance of your life. Remember that your hierarchy of values dictates your destiny. Trying to live somebody else's is automatically futile and can eventually be fatal. As Ralph Waldo Emerson stated, "Envy is ignorance; imitation is suicide." If we try to live by somebody else's values, we'll wonder why we can't stay motivated, but it's because we're trying to be somebody we're not and going against what is truly most important to ourselves attempting to be expressed outwardly from within.

It takes no outside motivation to live your own highest values, but it takes tremendous outside motivation to try to live somebody else's. If you put others on pedestals, you may even come to think their life is more important than yours. A lot of people on the planet do this and unconsciously become martyrlike.

Now the other side of the equation: You can go around self-righteously, thinking you're bigger, greater, and more adept, so you can arrogantly negate somebody else. Instead of injecting another individual's values into yourself, you project yours: "You should be doing this." "You ought to be doing that." This too is futile.

In either case, you're disempowered, and in that state, you won't as efficiently actualize your life or live your mission. You are unlikely to live and fulfill your mission while attempting to live somebody else's values. As long as you put others down, they're also going to occupy space and time in your mind and run your life. But they're also going to run your life as long as you exalt them. Self-actualization is not putting people up or down, but putting them in your heart and communicating what's inspiring to you in terms of what's inspiring to them.

Areas of Empowerment

There are several areas of life that you can empower within yourself. The first one is *spiritual empowerment*. An individual who's spiritually empowered might be someone like the Dalai Lama, Mother Teresa, Martin Luther, or anybody who has an intrinsically driven and expanded, inspired, or spiritual mission.

Everybody here has an inspired or spiritual mission in their own way. Rose Kennedy wrote, "My inspired mission for life is to raise a family of world leaders." That's what she was dedicated to and inspired by. That was her grand organized design. We can give back to the world in gratitude for the life we have received and created.

A second area of empowerment is the *mind*. By developing our mental power, awakening our genius, and pursuing knowledge in the area of our highest values, we initiate attention surplus order; that can enable us to have a more photographic mind.

Sometimes you meet an individual. Half a second later, somebody else asks, "Who was that?" and you say, "I don't know." But you've also met people whose names you've remembered for ten years. You don't forget the individual who is important and linked to your high values, but you instantly forget the individual who isn't. We get fidgety around people we can't relate to or have not linked who they are to our highest values, but we can hang around for hours with the people that we can.

When you're kissing your lover, two hours seem like two moments. While you're waiting for a train, two moments seem like two hours. When you're aligned with your highest values, time accelerates; it speeds up. But if you are going against your highest values, time decelerates; it takes forever. Our emotions distort time and space and disempower us. If we have a balanced perspective and we see things in order, then we're poised, present, and empowered. We can empower our spiritual life if our heart is guiding us and we are balanced and inspired mentally.

The third area of empowerment is *career*. We can empower our career by finding our unique area of contribution and service—our mission, calling, or métier. The body and mind are capable of fulfilling our most inspired mission, and we can master and express the necessary skills. In my situation, it is teaching, researching, writing, healing, and philosophy. That's what I do most proficiently. That's what I love doing. I can be in one of my offices or on my ship till three in the morning working on it daily. Nobody has to extrinsically motivate me to do what I love most.

Believe it or not, you already have great achievement, or what some call "success," but each individual has their great achievements according to their own unique highest values. Once a doctor came to me and said, "Dr. Demartini, I need you to help me become more successful."

"OK, where are you successful?"

"I'm not a success. I want your help to be successful."

I said again, "Where are you a success?"

"Dr. Demartini, you're not listening."

"No, *you're* not responding. Where are you a success already?"

"I'm not. I'm not seeing as many patients as I want to see."

"So where are you a success? Look again."

"I guess I have a successful relationship with my wife. We get along great. And yes, I guess my son and I have a great relationship too. I'm a coach on his baseball team, and we may win the pennant this year. And my mother-in-law lives in our house. Most people can't get along with their mothers-in-law, but we get along great. I'm also having a successful lay ministry at my church. Yeah, I guess I do have some success."

"Do you know that you have achievements or success already in the areas according to your highest values? You're not going to have any more or less. But if you shift your hierarchy of values, you'll have a different form of achievement or success."

He was comparing himself to another doctor, whom he considered successful. I asked him, "Where are this other doctor's weaknesses, or so-called failures?"

He reflected and realized the other man didn't have the same relationship with his wife or child.

"Would you trade places with that individual?"

"No, no. I love what I've got."

"Honor, appreciate, and love what you already are, do, and have, because when you do, you receive and achieve more to be appreciative of."

This man finally realized that he didn't need success; he merely desired to change a portion of the form he already had. If you change the hierarchy of your values, you change the form of your achievement or success. If you first identify that you have it, you won't go looking for it. If you go to the bank to borrow $100,000, first they ask for $100,000 worth of collateral. If you can show it to them, they'll give it to you. Similarly, the second you identify that you already have success, your life and the world gives it to you in the form that you truly value most. The second you deny it, you're vainly attempting to get something that you already have. You don't recognize it, because you're trying to create it in a form that matches somebody else's higher value system. You're dishonoring your own value system and putting theirs on a pedestal. Once you identify your highest values, you will understand where your achievement and success already are, because you live your life according to your own hierarchy of values, not theirs.

I'm not right for dedicating my life to the study of the principles of maximizing human awareness and potential and the laws of the universe; nor am I wrong. I just have a unique set of values. Somebody else may dedicate their lives to something completely different. They may look at me and think, "Oh, he's successful." I may look at them and think they're successful. Or we may think we are not and want to project our different sets of values onto each other.

The Double Edge of Love

True love is not only nice, kind, sweet, and positive. True love is both nice and mean, kind and cruel, positive and negative, supporting and challenging, peaceful and war-like, cooperative and competitive. Once we redefine love as a balance of life's many complementary opposite states, we realize that we're surrounded by love twenty-four hours a day. As long as we're looking for love in a one-sided form, we'll be looking for our whole life and probably miss it.

People come to me and say, "Dr. Demartini, I'm looking for my soul mate. I want them to be supportive, nice, and pleasant, and of course gorgeous, or handsome." The individual describes a series of one-sided states. That's like trying to cut a magnet in half and get just one side. Magnetism means embracing the whole magnet—the positive and the negative, the attractive and repulsive, the nice and the mean, the kind and the cruel, the pleasant and the unpleasant. "I like you" and "I dislike you." "Come into my space, baby" and "Get out of my space."

If you're supported at work and everybody thinks you're the greatest, your spouse may be the one waiting that will nail you when you come home. But if you're down, your spouse may be the one to lift you up. The purpose of a loving relationship is not just hedonic happiness or to simply support; it's to equilibrate and balance you—which helps you be authentic. If you're up and big on yourself, your mate will bring you back down into balance. If you're down on yourself, your mate will bring you up. Your spouse will squash you or wash you in order to get you into the center of your heart.

If you are addicted to the pleasure and unwilling to take the pain, you'll be thinking that your relationship isn't working while, in reality, it's working magnificently. True love is a synchronous balancing act. The one who loves you most is the one who's willing to lift you up or put you down and return you into your heart. If you get above your true self, you get self-righteous. Then you attract tragedy, criticism, challenge, and humbling circumstances. If you go below yourself, you get comedy, praise, support, and pride-building circumstances. The second we go into the center, we find that the one we love momentarily just unconditionally loves us.

Think of a family driving in a car. The mother and father are peaceful in the front, and the daughter and the son—brother and sister—are in the back, fighting. They're screaming, yelling, and poking each other.

Finally, the mother turns around and says, "Johnny, Anne, please stop fighting." A few seconds later, they start again, and the mother turns around and says, "I believe I told you to stop fighting." A few seconds later, they get back to fighting again. The mother says, "Didn't I tell you to stop fighting?" Again they start fighting a few minutes later.

The husband, who is driving, is building up tension. Finally he pulls over on the side of the road, comes out, and scolds the kids.

Now the father and mother in front are tense, and they're at war. "Maybe we were too hard on them."

"Well, if you'd done this and that . . ."

Now there's peace in the back and war in the front. As they drive further, the parents start to calm down. The second they do, the kids start up bickering or quarreling in the back.

Family involves a balance of peace and war, cooperation and competition, support and challenge, nice and mean, kind and cruel, pleasant and unpleasant, attraction and repulsion. That's not dysfunction. It's a perfectly understandable function once you understand that love has two sides and that each of the family members is consciously or unconsciously assisting each of the other family members in being balanced and authentic and experiencing the full expression of love.

True love surrounds us twenty-four hours a day. We can't escape it. That's a really great discovery, but when we're searching for a form of love with only one side, we will be searching our whole life for something we're unable to find.

In order to perceive love in any circumstances, it's important to redefine what love is so that we have a more balanced and realistic perspective. Buddhism says that searching for that which is unattainable and trying to avoid that which is unavoidable is the source of our suffering. If we're searching for one pole of a magnet, we'll end up thinking, "I'll never find this," for it is futile.

Another aspect of love is communicating through the other individual's highest values. Sales, for example, is finding out the customer's highest value or dominant buying motive and articulating the importance of your product or service in terms of their most important and meaningful values.

Loving someone in a relationship is similar to selling. Loyalty, trust, commitment are not what other people offer you; it's what you do to help them fulfill what is most important to them: their highest values and what they appear to do back in turn. You can rely on them to be loyal, trustworthy, and committed to the fulfillment of their own highest values more than yours.

If I am willing to communicate respectfully and offer something in terms of my partner's highest values, she's going to appear to be loyal and committed, and I can trust her to do whatever most fulfills her needs. But I can't trust her to do anything other than what's highest in her values. It's my responsibility to communicate in terms of those values rather than expecting her to live outside them or in mine.

This is not just true of your spouse; it's true of people throughout the world. The second I go against their highest values, they attempt to constrain me. The second I communicate in terms of their highest values, they will give me freedom. Anybody in our life that we have experienced that we think was not part of love—that's our illusion.

When somebody's supporting you, somebody else is challenging you. Go back as far as you can remember in your life and identify every individual highly supportive or challenging as you can. Make a list of them. At the moment you thought somebody was nice to you or mean to you, ask, who, at that exact same second, was doing the exact opposite. It will blow your mind. Nature has a way of keeping a balance of prey-like supporters and predator-like challengers in the social food chain of our lives.

Carl Jung, the psychiatrist and writer, discovered something along these lines and called it *synchronicity*. Synchronicity is the realization that when you are supported, you are also being equally challenged, and when you are challenged, you are also being supported. You won't be treated nicely without also simultaneously being treated meanly and vice versa. Either by one or many individuals, male or female, close or distant, real or virtual. You won't experience a one-sided event, but because you project your value system onto things, you will filter your perceptions of the world around you that way and conclude that there are such things as one-sided events. But this one-sided illusion is primarily due to you filtering your reality and having an incomplete perception and limited awareness due to your amygdala's subjective biases required for emergencies and basic survival.

The master sees both sides of events simultaneously, synchronously, in a loving manner. Victim consciousness belongs to people who see one side of events and refuse to look for the other side. They see the crisis without seeing the blessing, or vice versa.

The Divine Design

Scan through your life, make a list of every time an individual was mean to you, and then get present in that exact moment of perception and let your intuition reveal who was being nice at that same moment. The individual(s) who will be simultaneously acting out the exact opposite will be one or many, male or female, close or distant, real or virtual. You'll discover that everybody's playing in a magnificent matrix, in a highly organized and intelligent way. I call it the hidden order of simultaneous contrasts of the planet, bringing everything back into balance and bringing true and balanced love to its full expression. We are surrounded by love, and all else is illusion. When we wake up to the depth of that understanding, we can't escape love. It surrounds us twenty-four hours a day, all over the world. If we ask questions that bring balance and order to our perceptions, we will feel grateful for the order, which then opens our heart to love.

Physicist David Bohm said that there is an implicate order in the universe. The Reverend Gerald Mann also said that there's an underlying order in the universe at all levels, from the subatomic to the astronomic; humankind is in between, in the middle of that order. When we open our heart by seeing the balance, we're graced and inspired. We become purposeful, we make a difference on an ever greater scale, and we feel surrounded by love. It is in this state of full awareness that we maximize our most magnificent resilience.

Make a list of everything that goes on in your daily life. Write down anything that is not inspiring to you, even though you may believe you have to do it. Ask how doing that activity temporarily, until you can delegate it, will help you fulfill your highest values and your mission. Answer that question with accountability many times and watch how your state of mind changes.

At first, you'll think, "It doesn't. That's why I don't love doing it." But look again. It's not what happens to you; it's how you perceive it. William James said one of the greatest of discoveries is that human beings can alter their lives by altering their perceptions and attitudes of mind.

Take everything that you do in a day and ask, "How will doing this activity help me fulfill my mission on this planet, or fulfill what's most inspiring and meaningful to me?"

Don't stop asking the question, and don't stop listing the answers until you have tears of gratitude in your eyes. Because if you don't see the link to your highest values, it becomes friction instead of fuel, baggage instead of inspiration. It distracts you instead of focusing you. But if you can link what you're doing to your highest value, you inspire your life.

Next, write down every single item that is on your mind—personal, professional, financial, business, whatever. Write it down, and then ask yourself these questions.

1. Is this something I can do anything about? If you can, great. If not, become aware that you can't do anything about it and get it out of your mind; dump it.

2. Is it something for me to do or something to delegate? If it's something you can do, write down when you're going to do it, and put a date on when you will begin to take action on it. If not, write down whom you're going to delegate it to, and when. Take it out of your mind now, and put it on the date that it is wise to be done. We fill our minds with things that won't be done for days, weeks, months, or years. We cloud our minds and keep ourselves from being powerful and present today because we're distracted by the things we think we need to do tomorrow.

Short pencils are much wiser than a long memory. Take those tasks and dissolve the distractions by putting them into appropriate time frames for yourself or others, and date them. Have an electronic or other type of day planner that allows you to get to those tasks so you can be present and inspired about the things that are highest priority today. This liberates our minds from distraction and adds to our resilience.

So first, link everything you do to that which is highest on your values. Keep refining that process. Then do a distraction resolution by listing everything that's on your mind today and putting them into four categories: *do, delegate, dump,* and *date*.

I spoke to Mary Kay Ash, founder of Mary Kay Cosmetics, before she passed away. I asked her, "Is there any advice you can give a young aspiring international speaker?"

She said, "Every day, write down six or seven of the highest-priority actions you could do that day. Write them down, prioritize them, do them in their order of priority, and reward yourself that day with an addition to your savings or investments and that night with a sound sleep. That will help you fulfill your dreams." Whoever has the predesigned daily agenda rules the game, so you might as well have an agenda for your own life.

The Divine Design

I have a law called Demartini's Law. It says that any space and time that's not filled with high-priority actions will become filled with low-priority distractions. You are accountable for focusing on the items with the highest priority; then fill your day by carrying them out. By prioritizing, you increase the probability of living your most inspiring mission.

The next step to take to be more intrinsically inspired is to read and reread the statement of your mission or purpose. Every single day, read it, refine it, and keep reading and refining it.

My mission statement, which I first drafted in 1972, has been updated and micro-refined eighty times since then. It started out saying, "I dedicate my life to the study of universal laws as they relate to mind, body, and spirit, and particularly to healing. I want to travel the world, research these laws, and share them within every country and every possible reachable individual around the world. I want to become handsomely paid and live an inspired and privileged life." It kept evolving to the point where it's now an even more condensed, concentrated, and detailed statement. Whenever I come across something that inspires me, I put it in my mission book; I fill it only with objectives that are inspiring to me and that are congruent with what I value most.

Next, surround yourself with people who are inspired and read their biography, or biographies of other inspired people. Take advantage of opportunities to be around such congruent, authentic, and impactful people. It rubs off. This is another key to expanding your resilience.

Money and Purpose

Some say that if you follow your purpose, the money will follow. I don't say that. You have a hierarchy of values. When money comes into your life, you spend it according to that hierarchy.

Let's say I have a list of ten values, and the lowest is earning, saving and investing money, and being financially wealthy. The highest is my children's health and education, my house, my car, and my vacation. If I get $10,000, how will I spend that money? According to those values. Will I have money at the end of my month? No. The hierarchy of your values dictates how you manage your money. If you do not have wealth, financial independence, or savings and investments among your top four or five values, financial wealth is not likely to manifest for you. You won't get around to saving and investing because everything else is more important. You will be working for money instead of money working for you.

I consulted for a gentleman who made more than $6 million a year. At the end of the year, he was $329,000 in debt to the tax authorities. I know another individual who made $2,000 a month, saved $400 of that, and had more money at the end of the year than the doctor she was working for, who was making more than $6 million a year. His desire for toys, travel, homes, boats, and a luxury lifestyle made him spend more than he set aside for savings, investments and taxes. It is not how much money you make that counts, it is how you manage what you make, and your hierarchy of values will determine how you spend and manage it.

If you live by your highest values and you have a high value on financial wealth building, you could end up with financial wealth. Financial wealth will also require that you package your other forms of hidden assets and wealth into something that serves people so that you can earn income to save and invest. And the value of financial wealth building will enable you to keep that money. Only 1 percent of the population becomes financially independent, and they have a different set of values from the people who don't. Until you have a higher value on financial wealth building, wealth will keep coming up in other forms. These other forms may be in the areas of family wealth, social network wealth, intellectual property wealth, spiritual awareness wealth, business savvy wealth, or physical wellness wealth, or just consumables that gradually depreciate in value.

Some people say, "I know what my purpose is, but I also want financial independence." No. You only say you want financial independence. If your life is not demonstrating evidence of growing financial wealth it is not as important as you fantasize or imagine.

I was speaking to a group of 5,000 people in South Africa, and I asked them, "How many want to be financially independent?" Everybody put their hands up. When I asked how many actually were financially independent, seven kept their hands up.

That reflects and demonstrates that 99-plus percent of the population live in a fantasy about financial independence. What they envision is not financial independence; it's spending money on their immediate gratifying lifestyles like some of the unwise rich and famous—on depreciating consumables that erode their potential for wealth building. The individual who really wants to be financially wealthy studies numbers, probabilities, and statistics. They're working, saving a portion of their income, and investing another portion. It's more often a patient, methodical approach to financial wealth building through savings and sound investments, not an immediately gratifying emotional game of impulse speculating that achieves the results.

Do you have savings? Are you investing already? No? Then you really don't have a value in wealth building. You are more likely to have a fantasy about living a lifestyle, and fantasies don't get you results. Many people think in terms of yachts and houses and cars and gold instead of business plans, balance sheets, financial probabilities, and market reports, which are way more valuable items to know in order to be financially wealthy.

Again, financial wealth has little to do with how much you make. It has everything to do with your hierarchy of values, because they determine how you manage your money. It's not how much you make; it's how you manage what you make. If you manage what you make wisely and savings, investments, and financial independence are high on the list, you'll save and invest and accumulate assets that will continue to work for you.

As you save, invest, and accumulate assets, you also increase your level of patience and resilience.

The Laws of Financial Resilience

Here are some laws of saving: The wealthy pay themselves first. The impoverished pay themselves last. If you don't value yourself enough to put yourself on top, why would you expect everybody else to pay you first? The world around you reflects the world inside you. If you don't value yourself and pay yourself first, nobody on the outside will.

Whenever you receive your earned income, it's wise to set aside a portion, at least 10, 20, 30 or more percent, for savings and then investments. Automate these savings and investments electronically so none of your possible volatile emotions can interfere with your financial wealth building objectives. I call it "the immortality account." Its purpose is to eventually grow to the point where money is working for you more than you are working for money. If the money's working for you, you're its master; it's your slave. If you're working for the money, it's your master, and you're its slave. If you don't ever save and invest, you'll be a slave to money. The people who tell me, "Money's not important to me," will stay slaves to money.

I know people who value others more than themselves. The second they get extra money, they take care of somebody else. If you love to tithe and give to charities, do that too, but first pay yourself. You have an inner temple, and it is wise to tithe to yourself as well as to others. Pay yourself first and let it work for you so you are able to serve and contribute even more to others.

Next, take the highest priority action steps proven to build financial wealth and link each one of them to your highest values: ask, *"How will doing these action steps proven to build financial wealth help me fulfill what is truly and currently most meaningful and important to me?"* With each answer you write, you raise financial wealth building higher on your hierarchy of values. The higher you raise financial wealth building on your value list, the easier it is to see it manifest around you. Why? Remember the husband and wife walking in the mall? Her highest values were children's events, so she noticed everything out of the environment that has something to do with children. If you have finances high on your value list, you see more financial wealth building–related opportunities around you. If they're low on your value list, you won't see as many opportunities anywhere, because, again, your hierarchy of values dictates how you sense, decide, and act in the world.

Be patient in the development of your wealth. Some people want to get rich quick. The wise keep methodically saving and investing their money instead of impulsively spending it. Eventually it compounds. First it starts out in a bank or a money market account, then possibly in some T bills or bonds depending upon the current interest rates, and then eventually goes into maybe blue-chip and large cap stocks or even mid- and small-cap stocks or real estate investments. At that point, the level of risk goes up. It's not wise to go out and take a risky investment and speculate before you save and build some more conservative investments as a base. First save, then invest, and only then speculate. If you speculate without saving and investing, you will eventually tend to fall. But if you save and continue to build a bigger cushion, then invest wisely, and patiently earn the right to risk, the less likely the fall, and the less the pain due to any volatility or fall. Financial independence occurs when savings and investments grow to such a degree that the money earned through compound interest exceeds the amount you make by working.

There's an ancient proverb (which I'm making up) that says, "When thy purse is full, more money enters thy purse. When thy purse is empty, more money is taken away." Carry cash with you. Motivational speaker Jim Rohn taught me this many years ago: carry in your pocket the amount of money you'd love to make in a day. Carry cash. You don't spend it. It's not touchable. It's just cash you carry. Whatever you make in a day, carry it with you. If you walk around and feel the cash there, it's a different state of consciousness than if you don't. If you're down to the last dollar, it has a different impact than if you've got a big bundle of cash.

Wealthy people usually have wads of cash. What about credit cards? Not the same. Credit cards can sometimes get you into debt if not managed wisely and paid in full each month. Carry cash. Do not spend it, because, again, when thy purse is full, more money enters thy purse. And when thy purse is empty, more money is taken away.

Make a list of the wealthiest and most inspiring people, and read their biographies. If possible, contact them. Believe it or not, in many cases they will talk to you. Give them a worthy reason. Invite them to lunch to honorably interview them.

Create a collage, and cut out pictures that help you visualize exactly the way you want your life. Be sure to visualize doing the action steps and strategies to obtain it. If you'd love to live on the French Riviera or on a yacht, cut out pictures of these things and look at them every single day. Have a dream book, and set an affirmation underneath each page: "I'm a multimillionaire. Whatever I touch turns to gold." Affirm and visualize those images and the actions essential to obtain them. Make sure the words and visions of these action steps and outcomes are congruent with what you truly value most. Build the financial wealth first before extending beyond your means and let your passive financial income buy your ever greater dreams.

If you apply even a small portion of these principles, it could make a difference in your financial life. I know they've made a difference in mine. Financial wealth building is another magnificent key to, and ever greater degree of, mental resilience.

Thank you for honoring yourself for your own magnificence and believing that you have the right to have your dreams. You wouldn't be reading this book if you didn't. Just by reading these ideas, your resilience is beginning to grow.

Chapter 2

The Power of
Your Highest Value

As we've seen, everybody lives by a certain set of values. Furthermore, everyone has a value structure that is as unique as a fingerprint or a retinal pattern. This set of values determines how you perceive the world. No two people have the same set, so no two people see the same world. There are around eight billion different worlds out there. Because this set of values also affects how you act in the world, it dictates your destiny.

Your values can change, either gradually or cataclysmically. I knew a lovely lady in South Africa who had four children. One morning, she loaded up the car and went to the mall. On the way, a truck completely destroyed and totaled her car and took the lives of her four children, and she was the only survivor. In the morning, she had four children; she was a mother. In the afternoon, she was no longer a mother. That's a cataclysmic change in values. Some people can have a change in values when their children go off to college. Others can have such a change when they're laid off or decide to start a new business, or go through a divorce.

Your values can evolve as you mature. Usually up to the age of ten, you probably just want to play. Between ten and twenty, you probably want to socialize with your friends. Between twenty and thirty, you usually want to find a mate and a career path. Between thirty and forty, you're likely to want to start a family and find your own business path.

Some values change more rapidly than others. We could call those that are more sustainable *core values*. The highest is the most *intrinsic value*, which means that you're spontaneously inspired from within to do the actions that fulfill it. You require no outside motivation, no incentives; no one has to remind you to do them. In this area, you're automatically disciplined, reliable, and focused. Nobody has ever had to remind me to do my research or to travel and teach and write. Every day I do these things, and I'll do them wherever I am.

As you go down your list of values, they become more derivative and more extrinsic, so you require outside incentives to motivate you. You do not need to be motivated to do what's highest on your value hierarchy, but with the lower values, you definitely will require external motivation, which includes some form of rewards if you do and punishments if you don't.

Twelve-year-old boys who love their video games can sit and play them all night spontaneously. But you may have to extrinsically motivate them to stop and go to sleep, or to clean their room, or do anything else that is not a priority and inspiring to them. But you do not need to motivate them to play their video games, because, for them, it's a higher, more intrinsic value. Many parents try to persuade their children to do what they think is valuable, but they just run into resistance and defiance.

Motivation is not a solution for humanity; it's a symptom. I have no interest in business motivation. I'm not interested in using rhetorical persuasion to get you to do something that's not inspiring to you. I educate people about accessing what intrinsically inspires them so they don't require extrinsic motivation. Outside reward and punishment mentality is not the key to a resilient life.

Building Brain Resilience

Your brain has neurons and glial cells. The glial cells outnumber the neurons by about nine or ten to one, and they respond to whatever you attend to and intend to do. They neuroplastically remodel your brain's neurons and build, nutrify, and destroy nerves to maximize the fulfillment of what you value most. Your brain is an organ that has evolved for seeking and fulfilling your highest values. Like a tree branch, it grows to the sky, to the light. If it reaches the sunlight, it gets stronger. If it doesn't, it dies. Your glial cells will strengthen and empower any neurons that are acting and perceiving in ways that help you fulfill what's most valuable to you—your path to the light.

If you do not prioritize your life and fulfill what is truly most meaningful and valuable daily, your brain's subcortical centers prepare you for what distractions will arise for the sake of more basic survival, which ultimately acts as a feedback system to let you know you have strayed from what is truly higher in priority and most meaningful and authentic.

Your brain is doing everything it can to help you. It is the master governor of your physiology. Every brain cell is affected by your glial cells and your highest value. Physical symptoms are feedback mechanisms to let you know when you are and are not authentic, living in a state of congruence with your highest value, and when you're not. Many illnesses are derived from subordination to outer authorities and the injections of other people's values into your life—attempting to be somebody you're not. Illness is a feedback to let you know you're not being authentic so that you can get you back to your highest value, which your true identity revolves around.

The Telos

For the last 2,600 years, philosophers, and now neurologists and neuroscientists, have been studying the impact of the highest value. It is called the *telos* by Aristotle, which means the *ultimate end* in the sense of aim or purpose. Napoleon Hill, author of *Think and Grow Rich*, called it the "chief aim." Ed Tulleson, an early mentor of mine, said it is your most magnificent mission. It's what you're seemingly obsessed by, what is inspiring to you, what you feel is your chief aim, or your most purposeful pursuit. It's called the *primary objective* by other writers. The telos is so important that a whole field of study has grown up around it called *teleology*: the study of meaning and purpose. Fulfilling what is most meaningful each day throughout your life is the key to maximizing your performance and resilience.

The fluency and the flow of your life are proportionate to how congruent your intentions are with your highest value. If you're intending and attending to whatever's most important to you, you maximize the fluency and the flow of your daily existence. By contrast, the challenges, obstacles, and resistance we encounter are proportional to our incongruency with our telos.

One quality that robs us of telos is comparing ourselves to other people: trying to be somebody we're not. We're not here to compare ourselves to anyone else on the planet. We're here to compare our daily actions to our own highest values, mission and dreams. The moment we become congruent, magical synchronicities happen.

The Brain's Executive Center

The human forebrain, including the prefrontal cortex and the two cerebral hemispheres, is the more advanced forward section and layer of the brain called the *telencephalon* (you can see the etymological connection with *telos*). When we live congruently with our own telos, the medial prefrontal cortex of our telencephalon becomes awakened and illuminated. When we live by our highest value, we awaken the highest, most advanced part of the brain. The second we set goals that are aligned with our highest value, our telencephalon elicits mastery. We become masters of our destiny, not victims of our history.

When we awaken our prefrontal, cortical executive center, we initiate an inspired vision and see a strategic plan for fulfilling it. We feel called to act on it spontaneously, and we're not distracted by subcortical survival impulses or instincts or pleasures or pains. We're willing to embrace all polarities—support or challenge, ease or difficulty—in pursuit of this vision. When we can find meaning in our pleasures and pains equally, we've mastered life. We cease to be victims of our history. When we live in congruence with our telos, the advanced part of the brain maximizes our potential, including our sensory awareness and motor functions. One of the greatest things we could ever do is discover that highest value and set sail as captains of our ship, masters of our fate and pursue what is most meaningful and fulfilling. It is through this pursuit that we maximize our resilience.

To master life, we let go of lower-priority actions. To live inspired lives, we can delegate these actions and get on with what's most important and meaningful to us. As I've already emphasized, if we don't fill our days with challenges that inspire us, they will fill up with challenges that don't.

Challenges that inspire us create wellness; whereas, challenges that don't inspire us create distress and illness. You can work for eighteen or twenty hours a day without distress if you're doing something that inspires you. But the second you're doing things that are of low value, you will become easily bored or burned out; you'll get cardiovascular symptoms and lowered immunity to let you know you're not being true to yourself. Our hedonistic model of trying to avoid pain and cover up symptoms is keeping people from mastering their lives. It's suppressing our own natural feedback mechanism to higher priority–based authenticity and wellness.

To go into more detail about the executive center, it has a direct connection with the visual cortex and its associative areas, so we get inspired vision. It brings clarity. Have you ever been illuminated by a vision that brought tears to your eyes and suddenly seen how you could accomplish something? Your vitality in life is directly proportionate to the vividness of your vision. Thoughts become things. Visions become reality.

The second function of this executive center is strategic planning. It assesses risk and reward ratios to make more objective decisions and do strategic planning. As an old proverb says, "When the *why* is big enough, the *hows* take care of themselves." When you access your highest value, your purpose, your *why*, you automatically see how you can accomplish your goals. The hows, or action steps, take care of themselves.

Another function of this center is executive action: you more spontaneously execute the actions you have decided on. These show up as spontaneous potentials within the brain.

The last function of the telencephalon of the forebrain is self-governance. The medial prefrontal cortex sends nerve fibers into the subcortical area of the brain and calms down the amygdala (which is your desire, reward, and punishment center), calming down the impulses and instincts of the animal within. We have the same neurological centers and pathways as some of the animals, but we can moderate them and calm ourselves down. Instead of responding impulsively and instinctually to pleasure and pain, we can govern ourselves and see them objectively, without reacting overemotionally. The ability to reason, discover meaning, and self-govern distinguishes us from many animals.

The executive center allows us to be masters instead of being ruled by the outer world. When the voice and the vision on the inside become louder than the opinions, infatuations, and resentments on the outside, you've mastered your life. That's true mindfulness, which is also the key to having a resilient mind.

When the Amygdala Comes Alive

If you do not live by your highest value but by lower values, the glucose and oxygen in the brain go down to lower centers, the amygdala comes alive, and you become more impulsive and instinctive.

Instinct is based on previous painful experiences. It's designed to let you know that something is associated with that pain and prevent you from going through it. The impulsive part of the amygdala goes after pleasure. These centers were designed to avoid predators and seek prey; they subjectively bias your perceptions in order to keep you alive. As a result, when you're functioning mostly from that area of the brain, you have a more subjectively distorted or twisted view of your reality. You have confirmation bias and disconfirmation bias, which distort your perceptions.

Instinct is not to be confused with intuition. Suppose I said to you, "You're always nice; you're never mean. You're always kind; you're never cruel. You're always positive, never negative." You would have a built-in thermostat or "psychostat" to know that's nonsense. Similarly, if I said, "You're always mean, you're never nice. You're always cruel, you're never kind. You're always negative, you're never positive," you would intuitively know that that is nonsense.

But suppose I said, "You're sometimes nice, sometimes mean; sometimes kind, sometimes cruel; sometimes positive, sometimes negative; sometimes giving, sometimes stingy." You would intuitively know that that *is* true.

Your intuition tries to equilibrate misperceptions. When you're infatuated with someone—seeing the positives without the negatives—your intuition is trying to reveal the downsides—the unconscious and unstated truth to you. When you are resentful to someone—seeing the negatives without the positives—your intuition is trying to reveal the upsides—again, the unconscious and unstated truth to you. It's trying to unite and balance these two sides in order to liberate you through full consciousness.

External emotions, infatuation, and resentments occupy space and time in your mind, and they run you. But if you balance them, seeing the two sides together, you're objective: *you* run you. You're a victim of your history when you're subject to the emotions of the lower subcortical brain, but you have mastery of destiny and resilience when the executive center takes command.

Consequently, living by your highest values is crucial for mastering your life, particularly the topmost: finding what you're most inspired by and orchestrating your life to fulfill it and make your greatest contribution to the planet. Those who do that are at the top 1 percent of the population.

Once I was speaking at the maximum-security section of Krugersdorp prison in South Africa. I was led into a room packed with 1,000 prisoners in orange uniforms. I asked the group this question as my opening sentence: "How many of you, no matter what you've been through, no matter what you're going through, no matter what you've experienced, have a desire to make a difference on planet Earth?" Immediately every hand went up. Even maximum-security prisoners desire to make a difference.

The greatest difference you'll ever make is when you're purely, authentically *you*, with a unique set of values. When you subordinate yourself to other people and let their influence cloud the clarity of your own telos, you dilute your own capacity for making a difference. The real you has no competition, but the diluted you is constantly bombarded by competition. And the magnificence of who you are is far greater than empty fantasies of trying to live in other people's values and remaining part of the common herd.

Value and Identity

Your ontological identity and your teleological purpose revolve around your highest value. Let's say you're a mother with three kids, and they're all under five. If somebody asks you, "Who are you?" you will say, "I'm a mother."

You don't have to look for a magical formula to find out what your purpose is. Your purpose is an expression of your highest value. Your life is demonstrating it every single day. But when you compare yourself to other people and try to be somebody you're not, you'll cloud the clarity of that and think you don't know what it is. Even so, your life demonstrates it. It may not be what you fantasize and expect because you're comparing yourself to others, but it's there. It's smacking you in the face. I can make up a story and even lie to myself that I am dedicated to some objective or cause, but my life demonstrates what I'm truly valuing and inwardly pursuing, because my decisions are based on what I believe will give me the greatest advantage, the greatest reward over risk, at any moment to what I value most.

If you say, "I don't know what my purpose is," let me ask a simple question: "What do you do every single day that you love to do spontaneously, that nobody has to remind you to do?" You might say, "I don't know." Yes, you do, although it may not be what you expect, hope it would be, or fantasize about.

One lady in London who was attending my signature seminar program the Breakthrough Experience said, "I don't know what my purpose is. I don't know what I want to do in life."

I said, "What do you do every single day that inspires you that nobody has to remind you to do?"

"I'm with my kids every day."

"You love working and playing with your kids."

"That's the most inspiring thing in my life. I live for my kids."

"Have you ever considered that you are dedicated to being a great mother?"

With tears in her eyes, she said, "That's all I've ever wanted to be."

"Then give yourself permission to know that's your current primary purpose, at least at this stage of your life."

"Shouldn't I own a company? Shouldn't I do something socially?"

"I'm not interested in what you should be. Shoulds and oughts and musts are imperatives injected from other people that you're comparing yourself to, and usually admiring and giving away your power to. That's not what you're dedicated to. You're dedicated to the calling inside you and in your heart. You're presently a dedicated mother. Give yourself permission to be a great mother."

She cried, gave me a hug, and said, "Is that enough?"

"It's magnificent," I said, "because being a great mom is also just as essential in the world as any other purpose or calling."

You may also pursue the fulfillment of social values, intellectual values, values in business. Some have values in spirituality, and others have values in fitness. Don't let any human being stop you from going after your dream and fulfilling what is currently or permanently most meaningful and inspiring to you.

Once I was speaking at a primary elementary school. There were 1,000 people in the room. I asked the kids, "What's your dream?"

One beautiful, brown-haired twelve-year-old girl said, "I want to be a great actress," and the way she said it was angelic.

I walked over to her and said, "Don't let any human being on the face of the earth keep you from your dream, not even yourself."

The girl cried. A girl next to her put her arms around her, and they cried together.

Afterward, the girl's mother—who was also attending—came up to me and said, "Thank you for saying that. That meant a lot to her."

I said, "It meant a lot to the whole room, because I think you could feel the heart open when she said that."

Three weeks later, the girl and her mother sent me a beautiful picture with a letter saying she had gotten a role in her first movie. Her dream was to be an actress, and she made another step toward living her heartfelt dream.

My Teenage Turnaround

From the age of seventeen, I had a dream of overcoming my learning problems and going back to school to become a teacher, healer, and philosopher. I've had some challenges, but that dream has remained in my heart from that day until now. It has not gone away.

I had a setback when I was eighteen. I tried to go back to school, but I had learning problems and at first failed my first test. I needed a 72 to pass, but I got a 27. I started doubting my vision, thinking that maybe it was just a delusion or a fantasy. I really had a low moment.

Driving home, I had to pull off to the side of the road a few times because I was so blurry-eyed from crying so much. I realized that if I couldn't fulfill that dream, I wasn't sure who I was or where I was going. I had an identity crisis for that hour. Those with a vision flourish. Those without a vision perish.

I came home and I cried on the living room floor, curled up in a fetal position. My mom came home and saw me there. She said, "What happened? What's wrong?"

"Mom," I said, "I blew the test. I guess I'll never read, write, or communicate. I'll never amount to anything or go very far in life, just like I was told in first grade by my teacher Mrs. McLaughlin. I guess I don't have what it takes."

Finally, my mother reached over, put her hand on my shoulder, and said something that only a mother could say: "Son, whether you become a great teacher, healer, and philosopher, or you go back to Hawaii and surf giant waves like you have done, or you return to the streets and panhandle like a bum—which you have also done—I just want to let you know that your father and I are going to love you no matter what you do. Boy, we just love you."

In that moment, my mom demonstrated and I discovered the power of gratitude, love, certainty, and presence—the four cardinal pillars of self-mastery. What my mother said awakened something inside me, because when we feel love and gratitude, our executive center comes back online. I looked up and saw myself standing and speaking in front of a million people. I said to myself, "I'm going to master reading, studying, learning, and teaching. I'm going to do whatever it takes. I'm going to travel whatever distance and pay whatever price to give my service of love across this planet Earth. And I'm not going to let any human being stop me. Not even myself."

There was no turning back. Human will, human sovereignty, and what felt like divine providence joined at that moment. When you reach a point where you are that clear, congruent, and focused, magical things happen. There's no option. There's no wavering, no wondering, no uncertainties. There's clarity: "I'm on a mission now." There's a power in accessing and living congruently with your highest value. It spills over into all areas of your life. Since every human being also consciously or unconsciously wants to live from that state, it's a magnet to other people. It synchronously draws to you people, places, things, ideas, and events that are congruent with whatever you value most. Your innermost dominant thought begins to become your outermost dominant reality.

Slowly but surely, people started gathering around me, and I started to build momentum and excel. When there's no turning back, magic begins. That's why it's so important to find your telos—what is calling you from within. It doesn't matter whether you are religious or non-religious: it's a calling that transcends those labels. Thinking about that dream brings tears of inspiration and gratitude to your eyes. Your vitality soars, and the extraordinary you that's sitting inside the ordinary you surfaces. The voice and vision on the inside become louder than the opinions and obstacles on the outside.

You're not here to appease. You're not here to please. You're here to live your inspired mission, whatever that may be, and truly serve. Maybe it's raising a magnificent family, like Rose Kennedy. You have a dream inside you, and it isn't small. Every time you live congruently with it, a magnificent entourage of people comes to help you fulfill it. You end up at the optimal place at the optimal time to meet the optimal people. And every time you do, it expands naturally, as does your resilience.

Whose Brand Are You Living?

When you live by your lower values and/or other people's values, the amygdala comes online. It's impulsive, compulsive, immediate, gratifying, addictive, and survival oriented. When we don't live by our highest values, our lack of fulfillment that results makes us instead turn to filling ourselves with other things, like food and consumer items. We live through other people's brands instead of building our own brand. Addictive behavior is a compensation for unfulfilled highest values. It's an immediate, gratifying, quick fix. Immediate gratification costs you your life, but long-term vision pays.

Moreover, the second you live congruently with your highest values, your telencephalon comes online, and the immune system, autonomous nervous system, and circadian rhythms normalize. Your physiology starts to perform at its peak. Telomeres are added to your genes to help you live longer in order to fulfill those greater and longer lasting visions. Your physiology expresses the resilience and ingenuity you have inside. I'm convinced that our current standard healthcare model is undermining our greatness. I'll give you an example. If you eat too much—a big steak, a cheesecake, a bowl of spaghetti, a jar of peanut butter—you wake up the next morning with puffy eyes, snot, indigestion, headache, and allergy symptoms. You go to the doctor, who gives you some palliative pills to get rid of the many symptoms. They don't often teach you how to eat. Nor do they teach you that unhealthy eating is a by-product of a lack of fulfillment: you're over filling your body without governance from your executive center to compensate for your unfulfilled "telos" or "end in mind."

If you go to a more holistic and alternative health professional, they'll ask for a lifestyle history and find that you pigged out. They'll tell you that those symptoms are not disease. They're healthy responses to foolish actions. You deserve to have those symptoms, but suppressing the activities with palliative drugs without learning from the feedback they are offering is not the answer.

If you understand applied physiology, you'll see that those symptoms are expressing autonomic nervous system imbalances. If you perceive things as supporting your current values instead of challenging them, you become elated and infatuated, the parasympathetic nervous system comes on and creates its correlating symptoms: intestines moisten and outer muscles relax. If you see more challenge than support, your sympathetic system comes online with its fight-or-flight response. You create other symptoms: the intestines dry up, and the outer muscles tighten. You create symptoms in your body. These symptoms are feedback responses to let you know you've got an imbalanced perception in your mind. If somebody comes along and supports your values and does everything you want, whenever you want, every time you want, you can become a juvenile dependent on them. In that case, you'll attract a complementary opposite bully to wake you up. Bullies aren't your enemies; they are drawn into your life to wake you up from dependency and addiction to fantasies of an easy life. If somebody challenges you, they make you precociously independent and if they are perceived wisely, they help you maintain your precocious independence, authenticity, and resilience.

The Spanish Model

Chances are, you've been infatuated with somebody and at first you started sacrificing what was most important to you to be with that individual. When I was twenty years old and at the University of Houston, I was in a microbiology class, sitting at the top of the amphitheater. It was hot outside. The auditorium was cool, so when people came in, the cool air blew wind onto them.

In walked a beautiful Spanish model. I spotted her in slow motion, the wind blowing her brown hair. She came up the aisle and sat directly in front of me. I could smell her perfume. I was a goner. I started flirting with her, walked out with her, and started dating her.

Her career at the time was pom-pom dancing training at football halftime entertainment. I stopped my healthcare studies of the sciences to learn how to do pom-pom dancing, because I was infatuated. My telos temporarily went out the door and my immediate gratifying amygdala came on line.

Within a few days, I was already starting to get a tiny bit bored. After three weeks, I started coming up with excuses for why I wasn't able to attend her practice functions. I felt it essential to get back to my studying, because my long-term vision was to become a teacher, healer, and philosopher. Yet my immediate gratification was temporarily as a pom-pom dancing watcher. I became temporarily infatuated with this girl and injected her values into my life. I was afraid of losing her, because I was so enamored—you only fear the loss of what you're infatuated with. So, I temporarily started to sacrifice my own purposeful telos and live in lower values; I temporarily set aside my long-term mission and mastery for the sake of a transient infatuation. Within weeks, that infatuation wore off, and I wanted to get my study life back again. In fact, the speed at which you are able to go back to your life tells you how resilient you are.

I learned something from that experience: if we subordinate ourselves to anybody we initially misperceive to be wealthier, more achieving, attractive, spiritual, or intelligent than us, we will sacrifice part of ourselves. But I would rather have the whole world against me than my own soul.

Whenever you set an objective that is aligned with your highest value, you increase your probability of achievement, because your sensory awareness, your inner decision-making process, and your motor functions are at their peak. You walk your talk; you don't limp your life. And when you achieve, you automatically awaken a greater inner calling to achieve more. Your space and time horizons become greater, and you believe you can do more and achieve more.

A Pathway to Infinity

Our nature is designed to go from the concrete to the abstract, from the specific to the general, and from the finite to the infinite. It is innate within our brain to do so. When we live by our telos, we open up a pathway to infinity. We open up the abstract, the contemplative—the potential that we don't normally have in the finite, sensory world. As Immanuel Kant says, we have an immanent mind, which is deflective, like that of an animal, and we have a transcendent mind, which is reflective like that of an angel. When we live by our telos, the angelic, reflective, transcendent mind is awakened, and our capacities are expanded and more celestial rather than contracted and more terrestrial, radiational more than gravitational—broad minded more than narrow minded.

To go back to the twelve-year-old boy who loves his video game, he will eventually master it, won't he? The second he does, what's his natural tendency? To figure out a way of manipulating his parents to get him a more advanced and more challenging game.

In my opinion, this is very important: the second you live congruently with your highest values, you spontaneously keep looking for even greater challenges that inspire you. A spontaneously emergent leader will pursue challenges that inspire them and that serve others. It is this very pursuit that awakens your inborn genius and your even greater resilience.

Life does not get easier. It gets more complex. A single cell divides and subdivides, creating more complex interactions. The same for our lives. We're not here to make our lives easier. We're here to find out how much complexity we can handle and bring order to it so we can go on to the next complexity. Fulfilling our telos doesn't make us shrink from challenge, but automatically makes us pursue solutions to it.

Self and Materiality

Mastery of sustainable fair exchange in economics means mastery of living by your highest value, because when you do, you have the greatest degree of objectivity and equanimity. When you live by lower values, you have more subjective biases, which make you either more narcissistic or altruistic. When you personify narcissistic tendencies, you project your values onto other people and expect them to live by your values, which is self-defeating or futile. When you personify altruistic tendencies, you will tend to sacrifice your values for others. Anytime you're imbalanced in a narcissistic or altruistic polarity instead of being centered in an intrinsic equanimity, you automatically undermine your financial returns by trying to get something for nothing or give something for nothing, which is unsustainable.

The mastery of your spiritual and material selves is one and the same. Spirit without matter is expressionless. Matter without spirit is emotionless. To live an inspired life will require that you care about humanity enough to do something on a daily basis that inspires you, that serves other people, that earns an income that's greater than the cost of delegating lower-priority things. If you can't delegate low-priority things, you'll be submerged in activities that are less than inspiring and that devalue you. But you will probably not be willing to pay to delegate these tasks unless you're honored and inspired by doing something that both serves people and earns an even greater income.

The world of people around you will challenge you until you decide to serve people and do something that fulfills the needs or challenges of others in the world. If you do, you are rewarded economically, and you are free to live an inspired life. We can say no to outside influences that don't inspire us and get on with doing what we're greatest at, that gives us our competitive advantage, that is deeply meaningful and that truly serves. I'm very grateful that I discovered mine at seventeen.

Psychologist Lawrence Kohlberg showed that the majority of people live with basic survival impulses and instincts likened to some animals, avoiding pain and seeking pleasure. They're run by religious dogmas, by social propaganda, by businesses that tell them what to do and how to function and what to buy. In any area of your life that you don't empower, somebody's going to overpower you. When you're not empowered, you're overpowered. There are conspiracy constructs of the world that will overpower you if you're not empowered. But the second you empower yourself, none of those mean anything. You realize the world is yours. And instead of following a culture you begin to build and lead one. You don't see obstacles as much as you see opportunities.

The Playground of the Universe

I have stated to myself since I was eighteen years of age: The universe is my playground. The world is my home. Every country is a room in my house. Every city is another platform to share my heart and soul. No one can truly limit me or what I can do, except me. I wonder what would happen if we gave ourselves permission to do something extraordinary and fulfilled our path of authenticity. One thing is for certain, our resilience goes up.

You know you're really committed to something when you listen to and apply the feedback from your own daily actions to see if you're making progress, and you're not afraid of facing what you find—the truth of what you do. With real goals, you don't want to believe in fantasies; you want to refine your goals and learn how to master them even further, more objectively and metrically.

A true goal or objective is balanced—not one-sided fantasies, which create anxieties and fears. The second we set a goal that's a one-sided, philic fantasy, we create in our mind its complementary opposite and corresponding phobic nightmare to let us know it's imbalanced; it's not complete. That's the amygdala in full run—trying to get pleasure without pain. The executive center and more objective part of the mind knows to set a goal that's balanced and knows it will have rewards and risks. These can be mitigated with strategic planning, which comes up with ways to calm down the fantasy rewards and mitigate the risks and turn them into true strategic opportunities. That's the executive center in full force.

My former girlfriend Trish, who's an award-winning engineer and industrialist in Cape Town, South Africa, found a couple of thousand people in a rural township that had no jobs; there was a very high percentage of unemployment. She thought, "That's a challenge. What can I do about it?" She looked at an aerial view of the area to look at the resources there. She found a train track within three miles, and she thought, "I wonder if I could reroute the train and put a rail that comes right into the area? What if I created a company building railroad commuter cars and engines and employed these people as a social initiative?" She did that in three locations. She built a multi-multimillion-dollar company because she cared about and set out to serve humanity.

I was having dinner in Ireland with a lovely gentleman who has climbed Mount Everest four times and the seven tallest peaks on the planet twice. He has hiked by foot to the North and South Poles and has lived with aboriginal people in countries where nobody from the Western world has even been before. He's an adventurer, and he was telling me with tears in his eyes that that's what he's loved doing since he was a boy. Being an adventurer is all he has ever wanted to do. He came up with a plan for conquering his anxieties and fears. Whenever he conquers a fear, he finds another and tries to figure out a way of conquering it. That's his strategy, and he inspires millions of people. He's done extraordinary things. His pursuit is to find his biggest fear, conquer it, and go on to the next one. That's his life. He's made a fortune doing it. His name is Pat Falvey, and he is an inspiring adventurer and leader.

Individuals who can see things as *on* the way, not *in* the way, have nothing in their way. They are resilient to whatever happens. They know what catalyzes genius, innovation, creativity, and novel solutions to human problems. It's not the easy life that creates innovation or allows you to wake up your genius. It is the resilient-minded life developed through pursuing challenges that inspires you.

When I was eighteen, I made a commitment to master my life. I didn't quite know what that fully meant at the time, but I now know that mastering your life means waking up your natural, creative, innovative genius to come up with original ideas to serve humanity. I didn't want to live subordinate to the outer world; I want to create something inspiring for the outer world.

I believe deep inside you do too. I believe you have an innate calling to do something amazing on the planet—to make a difference. You dream about it, but it's the comparison of ourselves to other people that often stops us. If instead we compare our daily actions to our own highest value driven inspirations, amazing things emerge.

Your self-worth skyrockets the moment you are congruent and authentic. If I started a cupcake baking and delivery business, I would probably not excel, because cooking and driving aren't my things. If you're a cat and you expect to swim like a fish, or if you're a fish and expect to climb like a cat, you're going to think there's something wrong with you.

You will lower your deserve level, your self-confidence, and your creations, innovations, and accomplishments the second you try to live somebody else's life. We're not here to live in the shadows of anyone. We're here to stand on the shoulders of giants—those who permitted themselves to do something extraordinary. At the level of the essence, of your authentic soul, nothing's missing in you, but at the level of your more illusive senses, things appear to be missing. When you perceive and think there's something missing within you or others, you judge and momentarily shrink your potential.

As Mary Kay Ash once counseled me: every single day, write down the six or seven highest-priority actions you can do today—not projects that take weeks, but action steps you get done today. If you get them all done halfway through the day, add one more. When you get that done, add one more, but don't allow yourself to be overwhelmed with unachieved goals. Just stick to the highest-priority actions you can do. Keep a record of them, and discover the highest and most consistent of these highest priorities. Discover the one item that you are here to master, and master the art of delegating the rest. Your degree of resilience will begin to rise.

You may not desire to run a business. You may desire to raise a family. If you're going to be doing that and you're going to be married to the individual that's running a business, you serve them by being the greatest you; that inspires them to build their business to serve humanity. You will not live an inspired life unless you're serving people directly or indirectly, because there is no maximizing of meaning and fulfillment until we do. The brain is set up with sensory and motor cortices. The sensory cortex is for receiving rewards, the motor cortex for giving services. The word *deserve* comes from *serve*.

Shining Star

Once at a conference, a lovely family came up to me after my speech—a couple with three kids. One daughter was fourteen, and she said, "I have something for you. It's a DVD that I want you to have."

"Did you produce this?" I asked.

"I did."

I said thank you, and put it in my pocket. Later that night, I was at the Las Vegas airport, and I put her DVD into my computer. It was of a magnificent performance of the song "Shining Star" that she had choreographed, sung, and danced as a thirteen-year-old, using her school as a backdrop. Her name is Victoria Amaral; you can find her video online.

When Victoria was nine years old, her father had attended one of my presentations and bought every CD, DVD, and book that I had. He went home and started listening to them. Victoria listened to them, too, from the back seat of a car, and the message sank in.

The girl went to her father and said, "Daddy, I know what my purpose and mission is. I want to be a great actress and singer and performer, so I want to take special classes. I want to do whatever it takes to do that." She wrote out her mission statement and her goals and focused on them. She started to own the traits of the greats and find out that what she saw that was great in other people was also inside her. It's a gold mine: I've seen amazing things happen in young or older people's lives when they learn this tool.

This lovely young girl started applying this principle. She took every class she could, and she watched videos of actors and choreographers. She was on a mission.

I'm convinced that the children of today, who are eating sweets and playing to escape that first decade, are not doing that because it's what they're designed to do; it's a symptom of their highest value repressions, not their expressions. When a child is enabled to live according to their highest values very early, they do extraordinary things right from the beginning. They don't want to just play and escape. They don't want to just eat sweets. They want to get on with their mission. I've seen it in very young children; it's very inspiring to watch.

I watched that video, and I wrote a little email back thanking her and encouraging her to go for it. Later that year, I was in San Francisco teaching my Breakthrough Experience workshop, and her father attended. Victoria and her mother wanted to come, but she had a performance that weekend. But they stopped by before the program began and Victoria came up and handed me, not a DVD, but a letter. When I opened it up, I saw that it was an amazing lucrative business deal from Disney. Later it went to an even greater deal. I really don't know what the limit of a congruent and inspired human being is. All I know is that when people become congruent, extraordinary things begin to happen.

The Traits of the Greats

Would you agree that Elon Musk is doing things that are outside the normal box? Would you see that Richard Branson has done things that are outside the normal box? We can identify what we may admire in them and then wisely look within ourselves with reflective eyes and find out where we have those same behaviors and qualities inside us. Once we realize that we are not here to be deflective through comparison and judgment, and put people on pedestals or in pits, we are here to be reflective through introspection and love. When we do we begin to wake up the awareness to what we already have within. Then we will begin to stand on the shoulders of giants. We'll live in a new playing field of possibility. We'll give ourselves permission to do ever more extraordinary things.

I'm amazed at the opportunities that fly into my life week after week because I take the time to reflectively own these traits of the greats. Every weekend when I do the Breakthrough Experience, I have people who think they're missing behaviors and talents, and I prove to them that those things are not missing. They are just in another form that is unique to them and that are in line with their highest values.

Infatuation, resentment, pride, shame, guilt—any polarized emotion that comes from the amygdala—if not wisely interpreted and used as feedback—can stop you from living with mastery and being guided by your executive center. I present the Breakthrough Experience to train people how to govern their amygdala's emotionally reactive impulses and instincts so they can do something more strategic, meaningful, and extraordinary.

The questions we ask ourselves will determine how we see any situation. Don't ask, why is this happening to me?

Ask, how is this helping me fulfill my highest values? Most people go around and say, how can I afford that, instead of saying, how can I become handsomely or beautifully paid to be, do, or have that or how can I make another million dollars fulfilling that?

I train people to ask new sets of questions in order to see a new life. Your deserve level will be exactly proportional to your degree of congruence. I don't know of anything I could do more than help people find out their highest values and help them orchestrate their life as a symphony centered on those values—particularly their most inspiring telos.

The Demartini Method

One gentleman at a session of my Breakthrough Experience in London was blocked in business and finance because he despised his father for something that had happened twenty-five years before. He had not talked to him for more than twenty-five years. Yet he admired his father's integrity in other areas. The part he despised was the conscious part. The unconscious part was the part he admired.

Because of splits of this kind, most of your decisions are run through the subconsciously stored splits of the conscious and unconscious portions of your mind instead of your superconscious mind, sometimes called the wisdom of your soul. Unless the conscious and the unconscious are integrated into full consciousness, they will divide you and run your life.

In the Breakthrough Experience, this gentleman did a process that I call the Demartini Method on his father, and he worked very diligently on it. Essentially it involves taking an individual or authority figure with whom you have some emotional difficulty, seeing both their positive and negative behavioral traits, and owning them in yourself. It was a toughie. He resented his father, and he was having difficulty owning the traits. He was consciously self-righteous in relationship to one trait within his father: "I swore and prayed that I would never be like that." And he was also unconsciously minimizing himself in relationship to another trait he admired about his father. But it was important for him to own both of these despised and admired traits, because until you can own both your hero and your villain, it is difficult to be authentic and a leader. You don't need to get rid of half of yourself in order to be a master. But you would be well advised to own all sides of yourself and know there's a place for all parts of you.

At the completion of the Demartini Method, this gentleman owned the despised and admired traits of his father and neutralized the emotional charges he had on them. He became more fully conscious and his heart opened up, he had a tear of inspiration and gratitude in his eye, and he wanted to communicate his newly awakened appreciation with his father. At that moment, his cell phone got a text from his father—after twenty-five years. We seem to have some form of quantum entangled communication system that even physicists who attend find it hard to comprehend; I call it the matrix.

Anything that we haven't loved will run our lives until we love it. Anything that we're not grateful for will run our lives until we're grateful for it. Anything that we judge runs our life until we transcend the judgment. We cannot have our greatest self-worth while blocking our love for the people around us. When we finally love, we make the difference without having to make the difference—not because we need to fix anything, but because we automatically see things in order. Whoever has the greatest order in their perception transforms the planet the most and becomes a leader.

Special Knowledge

I'm sometimes asked whether it's of value to have specialized degrees or training. I'm a firm believer that you want to be inclusive, not exclusive, in your learning and learn everything you can in every field you can that will be of value to your most inspiring cause, or mission.

I have a facilitator who went through my Demartini Method training program at age ten. He's now nearly twenty-one, and sometimes consults with leading figures. He has read nearly 15,000 books. He's a savant, and he's one of my great facilitators, but he doesn't have any formal degrees, because he's way beyond any school. I can't say that formal education is absolutely essential for everyone, but I say learn everything you can. Gain specialized knowledge in what you want to master, and learn it until you reach the cutting edge. If you spend thirty minutes a day reading with concentrated focus, you can be at the cutting edge at the end of seven years.

When I was in professional school, I studied neurology; I devoured every book that I could find on the subject. The neurology professor gave me a test. I wrote these answers: "A, according to so and so" or "B, according to so and so; obsolete answer." I wrote in answers that weren't on the test, and he failed me. I went to his office and said, "What on earth did you fail me for?"

"You can't put answers like that on a test."

I said, "Who are you to tell me what I can't do?" I brought in a box of forty-five neurology texts and marked them with little pieces of paper and said, "You're not my only authority. I'm going to use these authorities; I'm going to stand on their shoulders and transcend them." I came here to learn neurology, not just limit my knowledge and pass an outdated test.

He said, "I didn't know you were that serious a student. I thought you were playing a game with me." He then placed me out of his class and gave me the credit, and when he got sick, he asked me to teach the class. So don't let the standard of any school on the planet stop you from exceeding it. Keep learning and set an even greater standard.

Not Number One

Relationships strive for androgyny. If you're really polarized toward intellectual pursuits, business savvy, and wealth building, you'll probably attract a mate who's focused on babies, socializing, beauty, and shopping. If your wife's highest value is children and family, you will probably have a highest value on business; otherwise, they can't be fed.

Realize that you're not going to have the same values as your mate. If any two people are exactly the same, one of them is not necessary. The purpose of marriage is not immediate gratifying hedonistic happiness. The purpose of marriage is to find somebody you can delegate low-priority things to. I'm joking, but just know this: if you have beautiful children, somebody's going to focus on them—hopefully either your spouse or you and one of you will probably take on the accountability of paying the bills, even though both individuals may participate in varying degrees of both sides of the androgyny equation.

Many people live in a fantasy, thinking that they want a mate who makes them number one. Once I had a woman in a workshop. Her mate made her number one, and guess what? She wanted to metaphorically kill him, because he wanted to be around her twenty-four hours a day, make love with her, spend time with her, hug her, call her, and hold her. She couldn't get anything done.

I told her, "You don't want a guy that makes you number one. You want a guy who makes you about number four. You want him to have a job. That's number one. Some cash flow. That's number two, right? A few other things may be number three.

"Number three or four is more of an ideal place to be. Not below that, not above, because if he makes you number one, you'll be smothered and your freedom could be curtailed, and you may be paying all the bills. You want to put each other around three, four, or five. That's a more functional relationship, because your specialties are valuable to you." Androgyny will automatically make sure that production and reproduction balance in the family dynamic.

Again, the quality of your life is based on the quality of the questions you ask. "How is your spouse's highest value helping you fulfill what is most important to you?" Answer that question at least thirty or forty times to see that what your spouse is doing is serving you, so you can be thankful for that individual and not try to fix or constantly change them. Then your spouse can wisely do the same back to you. If you can't see how what your spouse is dedicated to is serving you and your spouse can't see how what you're dedicated to is serving them, you will have little to no respectful dialogue. You will have an alternating monologue, and the relationship could be on the brink.

It's futile thinking your values are right and expect somebody else to live in them instead of communicating your highest values in terms of theirs, or what inspires them. When you're married, your spouse is like a client, or a customer. If you don't learn how to communicate to and fulfill a customer's highest values, they go somewhere else.

Chapter 3

Unconscious Agendas

One major factor that interferes with resilience is unconscious motives and hidden agendas. Certainly you can point to people you know who have said they would do one thing but kept doing something else.

As we've seen, each individual, regardless of culture, creed, color, age, or gender spectrum, lives by a set of priorities—what an individual thinks is most to least important or valuable in their life. Nobody from the outside has to motivate them to fulfill what is highest on their list of values: they are inspired from within to fulfill them. You will feel pride for anything you do that supports your overall set of values. You'll tend to feel shame for anything you do that challenges them.

Although nobody's values are right or wrong, most people think theirs are right and other people's are wrong—unless the other individual's values are similar to theirs. If so, they'll probably call them a friend. If not, they'll possibly call them an enemy. When somebody on the outside supports your values, you'll probably think they're ethically good. When somebody challenges your values, you'll probably think they're ethically bad. Your internal morals and your external ethics are connected to your overall set of values. That's why people sometimes relate or confuse values with morals and ethics.

Theory X and Theory Y

In the 1960s, sociologist Donald McGregor studied management and found that there were theory Y people and theory X people. Theory Y people were spontaneously or intrinsically driven; they loved what they were doing; they were self-initiators. They did things because they loved doing them. Theory X people required incentives and outside or extrinsic motivation.

If you hire somebody and they see that the job description matches their highest values, they don't ask about incentive programs, bonuses, or vacation. They say, "Let me at it." They want the job. They want to serve.

By contrast, the individual who does not see how the job description matches their highest values will be asking about days off, incentives, and bonuses. They're the people who have Monday morning blues, Wednesday hump days, and thank God it's Fridays.

People whose job descriptions are congruent with their highest values don't think about taking time off: their vacation and vocation are the same. They feel fulfilled. Their highest value is their mission in life and they love to serve and become equitably rewarded.

Health and Disease

How do these facts relate to wellness and illness? Whenever you do something that fulfills your set of values, you tend to get an increase of chemical compounds in your brain such as dopamine, oxytocin, enkephalin, and endorphin. These substances are somewhat pleasure inducing and can be addicting, so you're drawn to activities that tend to stimulate their production. People's actions and decisions are based on what they think will give them the greatest advantage over disadvantage and greatest rewards over risks. These activities will generate the greatest amount of dopamine, oxytocin, and enkephalin, an opioid in the brain.

As I've noted, in addition to neurons, the brain has another set of cells, called glial cells; there are nine or ten of these for every neuron. These cells respond to how congruent you are with your highest values. Any time you do something that you believe is fulfilling your highest values, your glial cells will automatically myelinate your forebrain's executive center neurons. Myelin is a material that coats the axons (long sections) of your nerve cells, increasing the rate at which they will transmit electrical impulses to enhance your ability to fulfill your highest values. Whenever something in your own actions or those of others challenges your values, it creates a different set of chemical compounds, which demyelinate those cells, slow-

ing down their ability to transmit these impulses. Hopeful-
ness and helpfulness myelinate the forebrain. Helplessness
and hopelessness can demyelinate the forebrain.

Demyelination diseases often have to do with prolonged hopelessness and helplessness. People have found
that if patients suffering from Alzheimer's can find something that inspires them, fulfills their highest values, and
challenges them to feel self-worth in accomplishing it, they
can slow down the development of the disease. They can
alter the function of these deteriorating brain cells and
repair some of them. So our brain is adapting to a changing
perceptual environment. It's alive and neuroplastic.

Forty-four years ago, when I first started getting clinically involved in neurology, we didn't have the fuller understanding of neuroplasticity that we do today. We didn't
know as much about neurogenesis—the generation of new
neurons. We didn't know that we can actually exercise or
redevelop our brain. We now know we can.

We live by a set of values, a set of priorities. We're trying to fulfill our highest values. We open up to anything
that supports them, and we tend to close down to anything
that challenges them. We build or destroy or remodel our
nervous system accordingly.

The body tends to be most adaptable when we have
a balance of both support and challenge in life. You may
have heard the story of the Houston Medical Center bubble baby who was overprotected: when he was released from
the bubble, he immediately got sick. It's been shown that
biology maximally develops at the border of support and
challenge. As a result, even though we're searching with

our subcortical amygdala function for that which supports our values, we are also constantly attracting things that challenge them. If we had nothing but support, we would stay juvenile and dependent, so we attract events that challenge us in order to make us more precociously independent. Both support and challenge in equilibrium enable us to maximally grow.

The same is true in biological ecosystems with predator and prey. The prey is food that we use to anabolically grow and support our values. But the predator is constantly challenging us, attacking us, to make us adaptable and change. Otherwise we'd stagnate and just sit there and eat too much and lose fitness.

Again, maximum growth and development occur at the border of support and challenge, but our subcortical amygdala tends to look for support without challenge. We live in a paradox: we seek that which supports our values, but we also keep attracting that which challenges our values in order to make us maximally grow. As you've no doubt heard, similars attract, but opposites attract as well. We are attracted to things that are similar to us, but we also attract things that are opposite to us to break our juvenile dependency and make us grow.

Two Nervous Systems

Part of the nervous system is the autonomic nervous system, which governs physiology—your internal organs, your cells, and almost every tissue. It is divided into the sympathetic and the parasympathetic nervous system portions.

Whenever your values are supported, the parasympathetic is activated—rest, relaxation, digestion. Whenever your values are challenged, your sympathetic nervous system is activated—fight or flight. Either of these to an extreme gives rise to a distress response.

True wellness involves a synthesis of both. The balance of both support and challenge enable us to grow, and both sides of the autonomic nervous system, when in balance, keep us well. Wellness is wholeness in the body. If we perceive more support than challenge or more challenge than support, those sides of the nervous system will create physical symptoms to let us know that our perceptions aren't objectively balanced.

Every symptom in your physiology, psychology, sociology, even in your theology, is attempting to restore you to balance, homeostasis, and authenticity, to maximize resilience and adaptability to your ever changing and externally perturbing environment. Distress is the inability to adapt to a changing environment. So everything that's going on in our life is ultimately a homeostatic feedback mechanism.

The sympathetic nervous system operates primarily during the day, when you're dealing with the challenges of life. It activates the red blood cells, which carry oxygen to the body. It's catabolic: it breaks things down and oxidizes the body. That's why when you inhale, you activate the sympathetic nervous system. You bring blood supply to your peripheral muscles, and you're ready to tackle the challenges of the day. When this side is activated, it takes the blood from the internal, central digestive organs and sends it back out into the more external muscles, ready for fight-or-flight and running. At the same time, the digestive system runs down and dries up. If you eat during those times, you don't digest foods well.

The parasympathetic system operates more fully in the nighttime, when you repair and build the body anabolically. It builds white blood cells and repairs the immune system. This side activates mitosis (cell division). This process takes place mainly at night. This side activates estrogen and other hormones that relate to relaxation.

If you perceive and feel that you're more supported than challenged, you produce estrogen. If you perceive more challenge than support, you produce testosterone. Women under high stress can sometimes grow extra hairs and develop pimples. But if all of a sudden they feel supported, they calm down, their skin smooths out, and these hairs can even fall out.

One process destroys the body during the day, and one builds it during the night. To adapt to a changing environment, you adapt and recreate constantly. The body is a system of wake, sleep, wake, sleep; destroy, build, destroy, build—catabolic, anabolic.

Maximum growth, development, and wellness occur when you have a balance of support and challenge. If you look carefully into your life as a child, you will notice that if your mother overprotected and oversupported you, you typically had a father who was more assertive and aggressive to balance out those qualities. Or it may have been the opposite: you may have had a motherly father and an aggressive mother. Or you may have both parents who were overprotective, while your brother kicked your bottom. If your whole family supports you, the bully appears externally. Nature provides both support and challenge in individual life, in society, and in biological ecosystems, because it is helping life evolve, adapt, become resilient, and grow.

If you constantly seek that which supports your values, you remain juvenile and dependent. If you run from that which challenges you, you keep attracting challenges that are uninspiring to you. The wise individual will pursue challenges that inspire them instead of waiting for challenges that don't. If you don't fill your day with high-priority actions, which inspire and challenge you, you will automatically keep filling it with low-priority actions, which sap your inspiration. This occurs not just in business but in all areas of our life.

Most every symptom in your body can be traced to one of those two systems: some excess or deficiency of cell function governed by the autonomic systems. As a result, when your perceptions are imbalanced, you will create physiological symptoms to alert your conscious mind to that imbalance. The mind will store those imbalances in the psyche, or subconscious mind, in the form of impulse or instinct generating feedback responses as well as in the form of memory or imagination, until you're ready for the truth and synchronous balance of love.

Would you agree that you've had events in your life that you thought were terrible, but later you found out there was something terrific hidden in them? Conversely, you eventually find some terribles in what you think is terrific. In actuality, all events are neutral until we judge them with an incomplete awareness. In that incomplete awareness, we create symptoms to let us know that we are ignorant of the other side of the equation: we're seeing support without challenge or challenge without support. Whenever we are unwilling to see the full equation, we create symptoms to make us look for the other side and eventually set ourselves free from the symptoms once we do.

The individual cell responds as the whole body does. The cell has a cell wall and a nucleus. The cell is surrounded by receptors, specialized glycoproteins that respond to stimuli and hormones, neurotransmitters, neuromodulators, neuroregulators, and neurohormones. These hormones activate secondary messengers called cyclic AMP and cyclic GMP. Those little secondary messengers in turn initiate a movement of ions in and out of the cell, activating a series of enzymes that let the nucleus know whether to undergo mitosis, to build, or undergo apoptosis, to destroy.

If you are undergoing more challenge than support, the cell will slow down its mitotic mechanisms, because it needs to move its resources out from the center to protect the cell wall from damage, just as we do from our internal organs to protect ourselves on a whole-body level.

The varying ratios of those responses to our perceptions, whether they are mild or extreme, are sometimes labeled as illness. We have different names for illnesses depending on the cells or tissues that are responding. If you understand cell physiology, nucleogenetic physiology, and enzymatic physiology, you can get an indication of which enzymes are activated, which receptors are stimulated, which hormones are active, and which emotions are generating these responses.

Today we have so many high specializations in health-care that we don't have sufficient interdisciplinary perspective, so the specialist in enzymology and the specialist in cell physiology don't always talk. Yet it is wise to view an individual patient in all of those respects to appreciate what in their psychology the cell is responding to. Your body reveals what's going on in your perceptions. The more you study your body/mind's applied physiology and psychology, the more humble you become about the wisdom of your body, and its ability to adapt and what its feedback responses or illnesses may mean.

If you perceive more support than challenge, you tend to become dopamine-fixed and infatuated. When you're infatuated with an individual, you perceive them as being more similar to you than different. They're a friend. Remember I said your identity revolves around your highest value. You identify yourself by your highest value. If you see somebody with similar values, you can like or become infatuated with them, because you can identify with them. You can be blind to their downsides, their differences, and their actions or behaviors that challenge your values. But rest assured those differences and downsides are there and they will sooner or later be discovered.

You typically procreate during times of infatuation. I think that's because in order to perpetuate the species, we tend to be doped, infatuated, and blind to the downside; otherwise we wouldn't do it so impulsively. If we really knew what we were getting into and whom we were doing it with, we might not reproduce as easily. As I jokingly say, a few moments of activity can result in decades of rewarding and punishing growth experiences.

When you're infatuated with somebody, you open up to them; they become prey, like you want to consume them. Listen to the language: *sweetheart, cupcake, sweetie pie, sugar, honey, honey bunny*. At the same time, you are gullible and vulnerable to them. You minimize yourself in respect to them and put them up on a pedestal. That's what we call falling in love, which means falling into infatuation. When you put the other individual on a pedestal, you become afraid of losing them, and you may start, at least temporarily, sacrificing your own priorities and highest values to hold on to them, just as I did with the Spanish model. You can become almost addicted to the dopamine that you've generated with this infatuation. As a result, if the individual leaves, you have withdrawal symptoms: you experience grief, sorrow, and remorse.

When you inject the other individual's higher values into your life, these values enter your conscious mind. Your own values become secondary for a while. You lose contact with your true self; you attempt to be somebody you're not.

Here's a sign that you're infatuated with someone and minimizing yourself: you talk to yourself in imperatives: "I should be doing something other than what I'm doing." "I'm supposed to be doing this." "I ought to be doing this." Or in questions: "Why can't I stay focused?" "Why am I not disciplined?" "Why do I keep sabotaging?" "Why can't I do what I say?" "Why can't I stick to what I agree to do?" "Why do I keep making resolutions and not living by them?" Whenever you're not walking your talk, it's because you're subordinating yourself to some injected value from someone you are admiring or have temporarily made an authority.

Whenever you set a goal or intention that is not congruent with your own highest values, you will keep going back to your own highest values when you act. You also accumulate resentments, because you're not able to be who you are. Now you've got a split autonomic function: one part, which is conscious, is infatuated, activating certain physiological responses; another part, which is now unconscious, starts resenting the other individual, creating a different set of responses. You do not have an apparent excess function without an apparent deficiency somewhere else, but one becomes consciously expressed and the other "repressed" or unconsciously expressed.

Whenever there's a conflict between the conscious and the unconscious, the unconscious often wins. Even though you're consciously trying to live by someone else's values, you keep going back to your own highest values. Your unconscious makes many of your decisions. We say we want to do something else, but we keep going back to what we actually value more. What we say is not what matters; it's what we live.

Whenever we become infatuated with somebody, we can temporarily lose sight of who we are. We lose our own empowered state, because when we live truly and in a state of congruence with our own higher values, we have maximum potential and power.

Seven Fears

Here are the seven fears that immobilize us and keep us from living authentically:

- The fear of breaking the morals and ethics of some spiritual authority
- The fear of not being intelligent enough, educated enough, creative enough
- The fear of failure in business enterprises
- The fear of loss of money or not making money
- The fear of loss of loved ones
- The fear of social rejection
- The fear of ill health, death, or disease, or of lacking the vitality or beauty to accomplish what we want

These seven fears are processes of self-minimization as a result of subordinating ourselves to other people we think have more business savvy or achievements, more intelligence, more spiritual awareness, or some other quality. As long as we exaggerate others and minimize ourselves, we will disown portions of our own identity, consciously trying to be somebody we're not. Unconsciously, we're still living according to our hierarchy of values, but think we're making mistakes. In fact, we're not making mistakes in terms of our own highest values, only in terms of values injected from the exterior. There are no perceived mistakes inside the authentic individual with a whole human psyche. It's only when we're comparing ourselves to others and injecting their values and expectations into us that we appear to make mistakes.

If somebody challenges our values and perceptions, we tend to close down to them and resent them. As a result, we put them below us, and we get self-righteous. Have you ever been resentful to your mate, gotten self-righteous around them, and talked down to them as if they were less than you? When you project your values onto them and expect them to live by your values, you inevitably create frustration and futility.

If you minimize yourself in respect to somebody else, you will be ungrateful to *you*. If you put somebody into the pit, you become ungrateful to *them*. Thus whenever you judge others, and in turn yourself, and have an imbalance in perception, you become ungrateful. This creates symptoms in the body and the psyche. This is a less resilient state of being.

Ingratitude is probably the greatest initiator of disease in the body, because it's an imbalanced state of mind. It's an assumption that there's more support than challenge or more challenge than support. With an imbalanced mind, we cannot bring about autonomic equilibrium or "open the heart" with gratitude. Gratitude is a perfect state of equanimity, a perfectly and synchronously balanced state of mind. When we are not grateful, we're projecting our value system onto others in the world and judging them according to what they do or don't do that supports or challenges us instead of looking beyond and seeing the balance inherent in our social life.

Whenever we're not honoring this inherent balance, we create symptoms to let us know what we're doing. Ingratitude is gravitational instead of radiational; it weighs you down more than lightens you up. When we're grateful, we radiate out and expand our space and time horizons. When we're ungrateful, we contract ourselves, and we end up at a shrink. You don't go to a shrink unless you've got some form of ingratitude.

In my Breakthrough Experience, we help people identify their true hierarchy of values. A great percentage of them don't actually know. They are so used to subordinating themselves to outside authority figures and injecting these figures' ideals into their lives that they've confused their identities with their authentic selves and created illness to get them to be authentic again. Our physiological feedback systems and psychological intuition are attempting to bring our conscious and unconscious minds back together again, so there's congruency. When there is, we live most fully, we're most inspired, we have the most wellness and we become the most resilient.

Most of us have made at least a couple of New Year's resolutions that we didn't live by. On average, 80 percent drop out within a week or two. It's because they're not setting goals according to their true highest values; they're setting goals that are often one-sided fantasies.

Depression, in my opinion, is not a disease. I know that pharmaceutical industries like to promote that idea, as do some specialists—particularly the neurochemical imbalance model. But with the cases I've worked with—and I've worked with thousands—I don't find that to be true. I see depression as a feedback mechanism to let the conscious mind know that it is addicted to an unrealistic expectation or a fantasy. As long as the mind is holding on to a fantasy, it has to create symptoms as a homeostatic feedback response to break the addiction. The body is quite ingenious and does extraordinary things to wake us up to our true self. When we're living according to our highest values, we'll be more objective or neutral and we'll endure pain and pleasure, support and challenge equally. When we're not living according to our highest values, we'll be more subjectively polarized, and we'll seek immediate gratification, and we'll awaken impulsive addiction. Addicted personalities are by-products of unfulfilled highest values and misperceived ecstatic fantasies and traumatic nightmares. To the degree that our highest values are unfulfilled, we have a higher probability of initiating an addiction to something, whether it be food, drugs, sex, or alcohol. We're looking for immediate gratification because we don't feel inspired and fulfilled within ourselves.

People consciously or unconsciously do extraordinary things to fulfill their highest values. I've seen a clinical case where a woman actually initiated a terminal illness in order to get her family to come to see her. She placed unfulfilling demands upon, and smothered her kids with, expectations when they were young adults, so they moved as far away as they could; they went across the world. The mother used every guilt trip she could think of in order to get the family back there. None of them was working. She ended up with a terminal illness, and the family came.

I had the opportunity to work with this lady and ask her to share what benefits she was receiving from this so-called illness. All of a sudden, she realized one of them—it brought tears to my eyes—"Oh, my God, I finally got my family together. I've been waiting for thirty years."

Another example: I've worked with people with diabetes, and in my opinion there are certain psychological traits for diabetics. They like to make decisions and don't want to listen to your decisions. They tend to be self-righteous and bitter and project their values onto other people. If you want them to do something, it's often expedient to make it look as if it's their decision.

On the other hand, hypoglycemics are self-conscious people: they minimize themselves. When you feel challenged and bitter and puff yourself up and feel cocky and self-righteous, your blood sugar goes up. When you feel supported and sweet and deflate yourself and feel humbled and humiliated, your blood sugar goes down. People with low blood sugar tend to be on the humble, self-conscious side. They minimize themselves in relation to other people. Researchers have found that cats have a higher probability of diabetes, and dogs have a higher probability of hypoglycemia. You can't tell cats what to do, but you can tell dogs what to do.

One patient came into my office with prolonged and advanced diabetes. Her blindness was starting to kick in. Her legs were starting to get ulcers. She was definitely having neuropathies. The doctors said, "This is going to be progressive. She will have to take and monitor her insulin, and she will progressively lose some of her capacities."

I had previously had a patient whose legs were scheduled to be amputated because of diabetes and the accompanying peripheral neuropathies. We used a special protocol, and working accountably together we saved his legs, and his blood sugar came into a more normal range. We had

had such a change with him that I felt confident we could do something for this lady.

I presented the protocol to her, which was definitely going to be a lot of work: movement and exercise, dietary changes, dealing with psychological perceptions and expectations.

She looked at me, ashamed. She said, "Dr. Demartini, I hear what you say, but I can't do that."

"I'm very enthused about the results. I know we can get results."

"Dr. Demartini, I didn't come for that."

"What do you mean?"

"You see that woman out there, this lovely African woman who's wheeling me around in a wheelchair? She's been with me for eight years. She loves me, and she knows every single thing about me. She's the closest one to me in my life. If I get out of the wheelchair and live my life again, the challenges and responsibilities—and the loss of her—are much more frightening to me than staying in the wheelchair and dying. I'm running around to doctors looking for so-called solutions, because if I do, I keep getting my care and income. But in actuality, I would rather die than have to be that accountable again at this stage."

So you can sometimes see unconscious motives in these patients. The second you start moving them toward wellness, they come up with mechanisms to avoid it, because they're getting secondary gains and hidden benefits out of their illness. Many illnesses are conscious or unconscious strategies to fulfill various objectives.

I know a lady who got a stage 1 breast cancer diagnosis within two weeks of discovering her husband was about to serve her papers for divorce to go off with a woman who was twenty years younger. Her idea of losing him, her identity, and their kids caused her to manifest that condition. When I asked her some questions and uncovered her unconscious motives, she cried. She couldn't believe that she did that to herself to make sure that the other woman was not going to get him. The second he decided to drop the divorce, the stage 1 breast cancer underwent the rare phenomenon of spontaneous remission,* became fibrous and disappeared. We will endure extraordinary things to fulfill our values.

Addiction as a Label

Addiction is a label that somebody with a different set of values puts on you when whatever you do to fulfill your highest values challenges them deeply, and you do more of that behavior than they do. Someone who drinks as much alcohol as you and enjoys your company when drinking will not call you an addict; they call you a friend. But if you do things that challenge their values and you drink more than they believe you can handle, or more than they do, they will start labeling: "You're an addict. You need to get help." *Diagnosis* is from the Greek *dia*, "through," and *gnosis*, "knowledge," but it can also mean *di*, "two,"

---

* Spontaneous remission: A rare phenomenon in which a cancer is reduced or disappears without treatment. In breast cancer, a healing phenomenon has been reported where intraductal lesions are completely replaced by fibrous components.

and *agnosis*, "not knowing." The blind leading the blind. Diagnosis is not an absolute science; sometimes it is a label.

One of the most respected diagnostic medical centers in the world has found that only 50 to 75 percent of diagnoses turn out to be complete or accurate when compared with second and third opinions or autopsies. There are many false positives and false negatives. If somebody is eating too much, drinking too much, or having an immoderate amount of sex, somebody else may eventually label them as an addict. If enough people label them that way, they'll start to believe or buy into it. Have you seen people at Alcoholics Anonymous? They've sometimes moved from an addiction to alcohol to addiction to AA. They've been pivoted into a more acceptable form of addiction so they can function in society without getting labeled.

Recently I was working with a woman who was grazing on food; I think she had five plates while I was with her. She kept asking me to help her with overeating. Her conscious mind was saying, "I want to stop eating; it's killing me. Just look at me." So consciously you're hearing, "I want to stop. I shouldn't be doing that. I ought to be doing this." Notice the imperatives.

The first question I asked her was, "Let's now begin to identify the many unconscious benefits you're getting out of eating."

"There is no benefit."

"No. No human being will ever do a behavior unless there are consciously or unconsciously more benefits than drawbacks. You are saying that there are no benefits there, but deep inside there evidently are. We are now going to uncover them so we can take them from the unconscious to the conscious mind and make you aware of why you are demonstrating this behavior and show you how to transform it into a more fulfilling form. So let's find out the benefits of overeating to you."

"I can't think of any."

"Please look again," I said. "What are the benefits? There are benefits spiritually, mentally, financially, socially, physically, or in regard to career and family. Let's go around the wheel of life and look at them."

Again she said, "I can't think of any." What does that mean? "I don't want to find out those benefits. I don't want to discover the truth about what I'm doing here."

When you ask someone to look for the unconscious benefits and they say they cannot find any within a second or two, they are not truly attempting to look. They are wanting to hold onto their current perception and don't want to believe there maybe are such motives.

Finally, we uncovered the first one. It brought a tear to her eye. We found out that her mother, sister, brother, and father were obese. If she did not demonstrate obesity, she wouldn't fit into her family. That was a wild one!

Then we found out her sister, who is two years older, was bigger than she was and pushed her around and beat her when she was much younger because of the attention she was receiving. We found out that she was not going to let her sister push her around, so she made sure she ate more than her sister to get bigger and be able to resist her and push back.

There were two benefits; I was shooting for many more. Then we found the third one: when you've been obese and you lose weight, your skin sags. When she was dieting, the second she started to see her skin sag, she thought, "I can't handle that." So she started to eat to make her skin smooth again.

We also uncovered another fact: she tried a radical diet and lost a number of pounds. When she did, a man showed affection to her. He effectively enticed her to have sex and then dumped her the next day. So she swore, "I'm not going to lose weight again, because I don't ever want to be that vulnerable again."

That day, we uncovered seventy-nine unconscious benefits. That night, when she got the hang of it, she went for the rest and ended up with 150.

She came back the next day and said, "I really have no intention of losing weight, do I?"

"Not with the values and benefits you're getting right now—probably not."

"That's why no matter what I do, no matter what strategy I approach, I immediately go right back to doing it again, like a thermostat."

"Great, because your decisions are based on the greatest advantage over disadvantage, greatest rewards over risk."

"This is very revealing to me."

Out of 150 reasons, she had forty that brought her deep tears and deep realizations. Once we brought those unconscious motives into consciousness, we had something to work with.

I did not judge her. I did not label her. I did not condemn her. I did not say she was wrong or powerless. In fact, I said, "Time to hug yourself."

"Why?"

"Because you are brilliant enough to accomplish 150 benefits with one act—eating. That's ingenious. Give yourself a hug." She revealed how strategically brilliant she was—one act with so many benefits.

I don't make someone labeled an addict wrong. I don't find that to be productive. I honor them for their genius in gaining many benefits with one act. I said, "Can you see how empowered you have been in order to get all these benefits with one act?"

"I do now."

"Just as you have the power to do that, you have the power to initiate other acts. We can diversify those benefits and set them in different directions.

"How do we do that?"

"I'm not going to tell you you can't eat, but we're going to pivot the benefits into a variety of other things so you can do them or eat what you want without being right or wrong about it."

"What do I do?"

"We're going to come up with four or five viable alternative ways of getting those benefits besides eating."

We took the first one, and I asked, "How can you be part of the family and fit in regardless of size without eating? What else does the family do in common that you can do apart from eating with them?" We wrote down four or five different alternatives, such as watching TV and going to the movies or church with them. We looked at four or five alternative ways of being part of a family without having to eat or be large. Then we found four or five viable alternatives for each of the 150: that's 750 different viable alternatives.

In the process of doing this, there were duplicates, so there ended up being only forty actual viable alternatives. Then we identified the highest priorities among those forty: the items that showed up the most times.

Value Determination

Once those alternatives are listed, I took that information, and I used the Demartini Method of value determination. I identified the woman's top three highest values by looking at what her life demonstrated. I looked at how she spent her time most; how she filled her space most; what actions energized her most; what she spent her money on most; what dominated her thoughts, inner visions and inner dialogue about how she would love her life to be that showed evidence of coming true most. Where was she most organized? Where was she most disciplined? What did she talk to others about most? What inspired her most? What persistent long-term goals had she been manifesting? I looked at what her life demonstrated, because when I ask people what their values are, they often unknowingly lie. I was not interested in her ideals or fantasies; I was only interested in what her life demonstrated.

If I go to a corporation and present to the corporate leaders or management teams, they quite often distort and sometimes lie to themselves about their values. They use social idealism for marketing purposes instead of looking at what actually drives them, and therefore the corporation. I worked with a forestry company that wrote down their mission statement: they were dedicated to bringing the most cost-effective forestry, wood, and paper products to the country. But the real truth was that the CEO was dedicated to the company because he was so poor as a child that he had no paper. He made a commitment that no child on the planet would be humiliated by that again. His real intrinsic motive came from deep inside childhood. The superficial motive was the one that his slick marketing company came up with. It's important to get to the real driving value, not the superficial ones.

We put on a facade in front of people, but we have another life inside. Let's identify the real core values.

Back to the woman who had been overeating. Once I identified her top three highest values, I then began a linking and delinking process, whereby I linked her new viable alternative behaviors to her top three highest values and delinked her previous overeating behavior from her top three highest values.

"How specifically will now doing this first new viable alternative action help you fulfill your top three highest values?" Answer that at least thirty times.

Do this for each of the five viable alternatives sequentially.

Then to delink, ask: "How specifically will now doing the original overeating behavior hinder you from fulfilling your top three highest values?" Answer that at least thirty times.

So to reiterate.

Step one: identifying the benefits the individual is receiving from the so-called addictive behavior—in this case, overeating.

Step two: identifying the viable alternatives.

Step three: identifying the individual's true values as demonstrated in their life, because that's how they're making decisions.

Step four: taking the top five viable alternatives, the ones that show up most frequently, and linking them to the individual's highest values.

Step five: delinking or detaching the original so-called addictive behavior, overeating, from the highest values.

Step six: identifying the subdiction that's driving the addiction. There is no addictive action without an opposite subdictive action. Whatever you seek, you avoid its opposite.

Step seven: balancing out with the Demartini Method the previously stored infatuations and resentments, fantasies and nightmares, ecstasies and tortures and prides and shames.

As stated previously: You link the viable alternatives to values through questions: how specifically will doing this viable alternative help you fulfill your highest value? I have the individual answer that question over thirty times. Then, how specifically is doing this viable alternative helping you attain your second value, and your third highest value?

Then I go to the second viable alternative, again linking it to the top three values, and I do the same with the third, the fourth, and the fifth; I link the five viable alternatives to their top three highest values.

Whenever you link something to your highest values, you myelinate your forebrain's nerves with your oligodendrocyte glial cells, so that the sensory and motor function is now moving in that new direction as a result of new conditioning and neuroplasticity. That begins to occur in milliseconds. The second you ask the question and answer it, your nervous system is remodeling itself. I remodel the nervous system by linking alternatives to these highest values. Once I do, the individual starts seeing the world differently. If I can link these viable alternatives to their highest values, their perceptual awareness, decisions, and actions will move in that direction. But it's wise to come up with at least thirty benefits to strongly link those benefits to those highest values.

Step five is to detach the original addiction from the top three highest values. I go over to the original issue, say, overeating, as in this case, and I ask, how is your habit of overeating interfering with those top three highest values? Because if you condemn somebody for their addiction and they don't have a viable alternative, you create stress, anxiety, and guilt, which makes them continue the addictive activity: the brain is myelinated further to avoid the criticism. You have a viable alternative in place to myelinate the brain before you can demyelinate the pathway from the original so-called addictive behavior to the highest values without anxiety. Whenever you see actions that are perceived as drawbacks or that challenge your highest values and create added drawbacks for them, you demyelinate the old brain pathways and use neuroplasticity to move in the new and more viable direction.

I request at least thirty delinking answers by asking the individual, how else is this activity interfering with your highest values? Now I can stack up the drawbacks without anxiety, guilt or shame, because now they've got a viable alternative. With each new link I make to the viable alternative and unlink from the original activity, they're increasingly inspired for an alternative behavior; they can't wait to get up the next morning to fulfill their values on the new pathway. If they don't yet have that greater and spontaneous desire to do the new things, you haven't done enough linking.

This process can blow your mind. I've had people who were addicted to heroin for many years—six years in one case—come off it completely, without side effects or withdrawal symptoms. The withdrawal symptoms are not so much due to the drug, but to the brain associations made while you take the drug that support your values and your fantasies. If you dissolve those fantasies with drawbacks, the withdrawal symptoms diminish or don't occur. These symptoms to some extent come from the withdrawal from chemical compounds in the brain, dopamine and oxytocin, not just your brain's opioids.

Step six is, identify the subdiction that's driving the addiction. I haven't found one case of addiction that didn't have subdictions—usually one to five subdictions. A subdiction is something that you want to avoid in your memory because it is extremely challenging to your values and painful to you.

I had a gentleman in Denver who was an alcoholic. He came to the Breakthrough Experience, where we were dissolving emotional charges that he had accumulated dealing with his dad. His dad was an alcoholic, and was at times very aggressive and overpowering. The mother was his dad's complementary opposite. She was at times a very passive, disempowered overprotector. Whenever you have a wife that's highly disempowered, and a husband that is overpowered, you're more likely to precipitate domestic violence. This was a classic case. But after a few years of volatile family dynamics, she ended up dying from an illness when the boy was four years old.

The father was angry that now he didn't have a wife to take care of his basic home needs, so he made the son become the wife. He had to cook; he had to do the tasks that the mother had done. For the next decade, the boy was responsible for everything the father demanded. If he didn't do what he was supposed to, the father would beat him.

When the boy turned fourteen, he finally started to feel strong enough to gain his independence and say, "Screw you" to the father. He stole the father's truck, went out with his buddy, got drunk, got in a car crash where his buddy died, and ended up at the hospital.

The father found out about it, came to the hospital and said, "How am I supposed to get to work now? I don't ever want to see you again."

This boy grew up with these perceptual wounds or subdictions. He had to bury the death of his best friend deep in his mind, because he didn't know how to process it. His father used to beat him. He didn't know how to process that either, because deep down inside, no matter what the parent has done, the child still loves the parent and doesn't always know alternative strategies on how to deal with these challenging dynamics, creating internal conflict. Drinking became his way of processing these subconsciously stored perceptions.

Not knowing how to process subdictions drives addictions. You will rarely seek an extreme without avoiding something else that's extreme. The next step is finding out what those extremely polarized perceptions are.

The Demartini Method shows how to dissolve resentment and the emotional baggage associated with the experiences that we haven't processed in a balanced way. We balance, neutralize, and dissolve the subdictions until there's nothing there except *thank you*. Until you're no longer a victim of your history, you're unlikely to master your destiny, because whatever you run away from, you'll be running into. Whatever you condemn, you'll breed, attract, and become. What you try to bury, buries you. Whatever you resist, persists. Dissolving the subdictions through balancing the perceptions liberates the underlying drive for the so-called addiction.

Once the subdictions are balanced, dissolved, and appreciated through using the Demartini Method, we go to the next step: a series of questions about any overly painful and pleasureful memories, fantasies, and nightmares in your life that are imbalanced, and we bring them back into balance in their perception. Whenever you have a memory of somebody criticizing you, find out who—real or virtual—was synchronously praising you at that moment. Whenever somebody was rejecting you, you find out who was accepting and wanting you at that moment. Whenever somebody thought you were stupid, someone was thinking you were brilliant. It's an exercise of putting imbalanced perceptions back into balance. We're so accustomed to being right with our evaluations that we don't take the time to look for the other side that our unconscious mind has stored and is waiting for us with our intuition to reveal.

Emotional Baggage

When I was twenty-three, I wrote a book called *The Illusional Basis for Man's Health and Disease*. In it I discussed how no one ever perceives anything without a contrast in a pair of opposites. When you have a polarized memory that doesn't have its opposite, we call it emotional baggage, and it won't be freed until you bring it back into balance. Your intuition is trying to reveal to you the side you are ignoring to liberate the imbalanced emotion. It is trying to bring your unconscious conscious to make you fully conscious, authentic, and resilient.

When I work with you, if you are labeled by others to have some form of addiction, I ask you questions which help your intuition reveal unconscious content and motives to free you from emotionally charged content in your memory and imagination that is potentially haunting you. I help you solve and balance your mental equations. I may be required initially to use a form of regression technique to help you access content from birth to age five, but from age six to age ten, eleven to twenty, twenty-one to thirty, and so on all the way through to your current age, I can simply use the Demartini Method and see how many imbalanced perceptions you can put back into balance. As you do, you dissolve *philia*, which is addiction, and phobia, which is subdiction, because you don't have one without the other. As long as you feel evidence of a pain without a pleasure or a pleasure without a pain, you've set up bipolar addiction, subdiction, or philiaphobia systems.

The next step is to identify anyone—yourself or others—that you haven't appreciated and loved. Anything in your life for which you can't say thank you is baggage; it makes you a victim of history, not a master of destiny. I have people clear out any of the baggage that's sitting there. It is improbable to be addicted to something unless you have an amygdala based lack of fulfillment and a polarization of perception.

Yes, I know: I've studied the genetics of addiction, and there are many genes that relate to it. But many of the genes are turned on and expressed and turned off and repressed by perceptions and their associated autonomic and epigenetic expressions. This is new information coming out of studies of epigenetics.

It's very easy to fall into the idea that "my father was that way, so I have to be that way." This is a scapegoat victim mentality, and it holds people back from self-empowerment and freeing themselves of illusions.

We have tremendous power and potential inside us. As William James said, human beings can alter their lives by altering their perceptions and mental attitudes. If we take command of how we perceive things, we have a tremendous power to alter the labels we place on ourselves, as well as our functioning. I'm not saying that every case can be quickly and easily transformed this way, but in a vast number of cases, we do have the power to change. It is more often a skill at navigating through their conscious or unconscious motives.

When you understand the mind's functions and strategies and utilize them wisely, they can cause profound transformations in your physiology and psychology. When you're living congruently with your highest values, you have the greatest potential and great resilience.

I really don't know the limits of the potential of our mind; as Deepak Chopra says, it may be infinite. I recently met a ten-year-old autistic savant, who read a text on astrophysics in minutes and has photographic memory of a 400-page text. I've seen people who have had spontaneous remissions of their illness.

One doctor in Calgary, Alberta, sent me a patient who had regional ileitis, Crohn's disease, for eleven years. She was torn up inside—ulceration of the small intestine, bloody stools, cramps, bloat, and fatigue. She had internal conflict dealing with sexual confusion about her father. The mother had repressed her sexuality, and the father was playing out part of the repressed sexuality with her. The daughter picked it up.

Again, whatever the parents repress, the children are sometimes going to express. Whatever you condemn, you'll breed. Tell me what you condemn most, tell me what you repress most, and I'll tell you what your children may just specialize in.

In this case, the child was living out the sexual repression of the mother with the dad. The dad had not gotten past shame and guilt over a masturbation issue; he was charged up about that memory and was trying to work through that process. From childhood, she started to have regional ileitis, because she didn't know how to process the internal conflict between all the shoulds from society and the feelings she was having for her father and mother.

Using the Demartini Method, I dissolved many of the emotional charges. She opened her heart for her father and her mother and saw a higher order. She understood why she specialized in the career that she did and why she attracted the man in her life. She was in tears of gratitude. It was the last day she ever had any regional ileitis symptoms.

Healing Deafness and Blindness

In the Breakthrough Experience seminar program I presented in Hamilton, Ontario, I had an attending man who was in his forties. He had been blind and deaf from birth, but he was a chiropractor. Because he couldn't hear or see, he had heightened his kinesthetic and tactile sensibility, and he was an incredible practitioner, working with his hands. People came from all over to see him. He brought a woman assistant, or special translator, to help him communicate with hand and finger tactile communication.

In the program I asked this man, through his translator, who was the biggest cause of resentment in his life. It was his father. As he came through the birth canal when he was born, his head was deformed (which happens to some children, although later their heads usually return to normal). The father saw that and thought he was mentally handicapped. He couldn't handle the idea that he had a deformed or deranged child, and he knocked the child naked out of the mother's hands onto the ground. The father then left and never saw the mother or child again. Don't think children don't remember these things. I regress people back, and we uncover some amazing and later confirmed experiences. It's unbelievable what they remember. Some specialists believe and say that such memories are improbable but they certainly occur and many regressions have uncovered amazing content that is confirmable.

Most of the attendees finished the Demartini Method process in the workshop by midnight, though not him. He went home and worked by himself till three in the morning to process through the questions.

At three in the morning, an insight came to him. The word *embarrassed* came to his mind, because he had been embarrassed by his own nakedness when his father knocked him out of his mother's arms. All he could hear in the back of his mind was, "I don't want to see him. I don't want to hear him." He through some form of somatization* shut down hearing and sight.

At three o'clock in the morning, this man, through new associations discovered, awakened unconscious content from his mind and put a life puzzle together. He realized that this birth incident was now suddenly a gift, because it led him to the healing arts, to the skills he is known for, to

---

* Somatization: When psychological concerns are converted into physical symptoms.

much of the life he had today. He suddenly saw clearly the missing and balancing upsides to what was perceived to be rejection and all downsides. He was grateful; he opened his heart and for the first time felt love for his father. He started to say, "I am a doctor because of that. I have special skills because of that. I am who I am because of that. I now feel that that was not a mistake. There's a higher order to it." He was no longer the victim of his history.

The man taped what he was doing, and he brought it to give to me the next morning. The recording of his response was muffled, but at one point I heard a grandfather clock go off in the background. At the moment he was sitting there, being grateful and in an ecstatic state of appreciation for his mother and father, he said, "Oh, my God! Oh, my God! I heard the clock. I can hear!" A few seconds later, he turned his head toward where the sound was coming from; after forty years, his eyesight and hearing had returned. I have the tape. If you listen to it, you'll be blown away and will experience chills up your spine and tears in your eyes.

The next morning, when I walked in, some people were gathered around him.

"What's going on over here?" I asked.

"Last night, at three o'clock in the morning," the man said, "my eyesight and my hearing from birth returned. I can see and hear again." I had to sit down, because that was astonishing and inspiring to me.

But even this amazing recovery had its benefits and drawbacks, because his wife's identity was wrapped up around being his support. When that wasn't needed anymore, it created a major challenge for him that may have been as challenging as not seeing or hearing. Because nature involves a balance of support and challenge, there was a new support and a new challenge.

In any event, I don't know what the limitations of a balanced mind are in healing the body. I wrote a book in 1997 titled *Count Your Blessings: The Healing Power of Gratitude and Love* because of so many transformations in healing that I had seen.

In my mid-twenties I worked next door to MD Anderson Cancer Center in Houston, and I became friendly with some of the doctors and nurses. The head oncology nurse said, "When people come in, we can often tell who's going to make it and who's not by their personalities and attitudes. We have about an 87 percent predictability rate." These were supposedly terminal patients, but their conscious and unconscious motives often determined whether they were going to live or die.

Axiology: The Study of Values

Axiology is a branch of epistemology, the study of knowledge, that explores the study of values and worth. Economics is derived from axiology.

In his famous study of personality and motivation, psychologist Abraham Maslow said that if we do not have adequate shelter, food, clothing, and reproduction, we search for those things. That's called survival. I know what it's like to have very few clothes, live on the streets, and scrounge for food. I lived that way as a teenager.

If you acquire those basic survival needs, you go on to another level called security. Once you've acquired your basic needs, you protect them, and you don't want anybody to take them away. It's territoriality. If you get food, you want to make sure nobody takes it. If you get sex, you want to make sure nobody takes away the one who's giving it to you.

Once you have security stabilized, you go to socialization. You show off in front of your peers. "Look what I have. Look at the trophy I've got. Look at the house I'm getting."

The next level is self-esteem. The last one is self-actualization or self-fulfillment, whereby you realize that everyone around you is a reflection of you. We're not here to be above or below other people; we're here to be of service to them and help them fulfill their lives as much as our own. Where equanimity and equity reign.

Whatever is perceived to be most absent from our life can then become perceived as most important. If we think we don't have sufficient money, we can seek money. If we think we don't have shelter, we can look for a house. As a result, our values are based on what has not yet been fulfilled perceptually.

By another perspective, there are six different types of values:

1. If we have a void, we want to fill it.
2. If we have a question, we want to answer it.
3. If we have a mystery, we want to solve it.
4. If we have a problem, we want to find a solution to it.
5. If we have an unknown, we want to know it.
6. If we see chaos, we want to find or bring order in or to it.

We're constantly trying to make sense out of our world. We place a value making sense out of anything that doesn't make sense.

There are two aspects of axiology: other worth and self-worth. If I can fulfill your needs, answer your questions, solve your problems and mysteries, and help you tackle your challenges, I have a worth to you; I'm valuable to you. If I can solve my own problems, answer my own questions, fill my own voids, I have self-worth.

If I have other worth, I have a source of income. If I have self-worth, I will keep some of that income. If I don't have self-worth, but I have other worth, I will generate money, but I will spend it or give it to people instead of keeping it. If I have great self-worth, but no other worth, I won't generate income, but whatever I get, I'll hoard. If I have self-worth and other worth through reflective awareness, I will do both: I will serve people, gain an income, and keep a portion of it.

The True Meaning of Values

Wealth means *well-being*, *whole being*, because you're now whole. That's what I mean by values. Values are not necessarily limited to more classical morals and ethics: these social contracts and often hypocritical ideals are by-products of values rather than values as such. You will tend to open up to anything that supports your values and label it as good. If something challenges your values, you'll tend to close down to it and label it as bad.

Values may not have much to do with what most people think. If you ask people, "What are your values?" they'll say things like integrity, truth, and honesty, but when we get down to their true life demonstrations, it's not exactly the same. If you look at how they spend their time and energy, and the other eleven value determinants provided previously (see page 20), it's not exactly all about honesty or integrity, these latter two being social idealisms and in many cases moral hypocrisies.

Values have to do with what you spontaneously spend your time, energy, and money on. My highest value is figuring out the laws of human behavior and teaching. That's how I spend my time, energy, and money. That's how I fill my space. That's what I'm disciplined about. That's what I think about, focus on, visualize. Which means that I have a big void: I have a vast unknown out there that I want to understand and solve in my field. I feel like a child in a candy store. There's so much I don't know that I want to know. If I didn't have that void, I wouldn't have that value.

Authenticity and Vulnerability

I'm sometimes asked how to find the loving balance between infatuation and resentment. How can you open up to and be authentic with someone you care about?

We're not here to put people on pedestals or in pits. We're not here to be too humble to admit that what we see in them is inside us, or too proud to admit that what we see inside us is inside them. We're here to have reflective awareness and open up to others and ourselves at the same time—to realize the magnificence and wholeness of both of us.

In the Breakthrough Experience, I have an exercise: we take the specific traits, actions, or inactions that we admire and despise most in someone else; then we introspect and reflect and find out where we have those same specific traits, actions, or inactions in ourselves. If we admire a behavior, we find the downside. If we resent a behavior, we find the upside. We balance the slate. We look honestly within, and with whatever they've done, we find out where we've done it and whom we've done it to—to the same degree, quantitatively and qualitatively. If we're too proud or ashamed of what we've done, we neutralize it by finding the drawbacks or the benefits to those we have displayed it to.

Then we look at whenever someone has done something to you, asking, who has done the equal and opposite to you simultaneously to keep the balance? That makes you aware of a higher order or an inherent intelligence in the universe that you may not have been aware of before. Some theologians have called God; others have called the grand organized field, the implicate order, synchronicity, the equal and opposite force, the law of eristic escalation, the matrix, or whatever you want to call it. In any case, there's a field in life that keeps biological organisms evolving and growing maximally at the border of support and challenge.

A number of years back, I wrote a two-volume set of books called *Mysteries of the Living Cell* on the origin of life and cells and how they may have originated on the planet. When I was studying that subject, I was blown away by the magnificent and intricate intelligence governing the cell. There's no way you can study that without being humbled.

Once I discussed this with American theoretical physicist, mathematician, and biologist Freeman J. Dyson at Princeton's Institute for Advanced Studies. He acknowledged that there are potentially fields of intelligence at each scale in the universe: so far there's no way of fully explaining the events inside a cell through random thermodynamics. We would be wise to humble ourselves to the non-anthropomorphic intelligence that's potentially running the system. If we took all the Nobel Prize winners in the world, stuck them together, and made a supermind, they still wouldn't be able to figure out how a single cell organism is running. And yet 4.2 billion years ago, before even the so-called evolution of human beings, the cell was running perfectly.

It is interesting how archeologists can find a poorly prepared 2.3-million-year-old flint buried in sediments and describe it as a sign of early intelligence, and then turn around and state that a cell, which is vastly more complex, is not a sign of intelligence.

Chapter 4

The Importance
of Epigenetics

Professor Conrad Waddington is credited with coining the term *epigenetics* around 1942. *Epi-* means *upon*, *above*, or *outside*. Epigenetics deals with how the genetic code is influenced by things outside, above, or around the genes, including what turns the expression of genes on and off. Epigenetics is one of the most significant frontiers in the health field today, and it has extreme pertinence to our life and our resilience.

Initially, scientists believed that genetics was stable: the genes were passed on mitotically—that is, by simple cell division—to the next daughter cells, and so on. But they wondered, "What causes the cells to differentiate?" After all, if the daughter cells are apparently genetically the same as the parents', something besides the genes appears to be causing them to change their shape, form, and activities. Even though we have the same genotype, we obviously have different phenotypes, not only in our individuality, but also in the morphology of our cells. What accounts for this?

To explain this phenomenon, theorists had to come up with something beyond simple cell reproduction. In the 1940s, new discoveries enabled science to look at what might be influencing genetic expression.

From the Beginning

Let's start from where we ourselves as physical bodies begin. Reproduction occurs when two sex cells, called gametes, come together: sperm and egg. These cells are produced meiotically: that is, each has divided its two sets of genes into one, enabling them to merge. When they do, they create a zygote. This zygote is diploid, as are the cells of all life forms that reproduce sexually (except for sperm and egg, which are haploid: they only have a single set of genes, from the father or the mother). The zygote divides, and it creates daughter cells through mitotic division, duplicating the parent cell's genetic code.

These first two cells are similar to the zygote. They divide again and create a four-cell tetrahedron formation. These cells in turn duplicate into eight cells, whose division creates a cluster of cells, which develop further into first a morula, then a blastula. These divide to create into a blastocoel, which generates a gastrula.

In the gastrula stage (a week or two after conception), certain changes are already evident. At this point, the cell types are starting to differentiate noticeably. Differentiation is making different kinds of cells out of one. You start to see something that's going to be the nervous system, skin, muscles, and blood vessels.

The gastrula starts to differentiate further into the derm lines: ectoderm, mesoderm, and endoderm. The endoderm will develop into the internal lining of the intestines, stomach, and liver.

At the beginning of this development, the initial cell, the zygote, is called *totipotential*. That means it has the total potential to create the entire living organism, with its 200–220 different types of cells.

At the same time, the ectoderm starts developing the notochord and the nervous system. By the third week, a nervous system is already starting to form. By the second to third week, the cardiovascular system, the heart, is already differentiating. At this point, the cell is now *pluripotential*, meaning it still has many options, but not all. Each of those cells becomes monopotential—what we become at and after birth, when the cells are fully differentiated. They're now unique, and they're specialized. Now we have cells for all the functions in our body.

The initial cell is a stem cell: a cell with branches, which start to differentiate at each step. As this occurs, because the genes are the same and relatively consistent, the genotype is pretty consistent.

What causes the cell to differentiate? The parent cell and the two daughter cells exchange signals between them. These are photonic interactions, meaning that particles of light are used to communicate information—light-based cellular interactions.

The cells also exchange subatomic particles, which are positive and negatively charged—positron and electron based cellular interactions. Then certain atoms are exchanged, such as calcium, zinc, magnesium, and copper, causing the daughter cell to change its function slightly—cation and anion based cellular interactions. As the cell further differentiates, it produces amino acid transmitters and signal molecules, which are also initially called *morphogens*, because they're changing the morphology, or form, of the cell. They're also called *signals*. In any case, when a cell starts to divide and differentiate, it activates a unique set of responses and new communication signals with the next cell.

Initially the first cell interacts with itself—which is called an autocrine function. Then it interacts with adjacent cells—which is called a juxtracrine interaction or function. As this process gets more complex and to cells farther away but still nearby, it is called a *paracrine function*. *Para-* means *near*. It means there's a connection next to the cell. In addition, there are junctions and fibers that hold these cells together. They send signals through the cell wall, communicating information between cells.

As the cells differentiate, they produce many kinds of interactions, which at one time we couldn't see even with a microscope. Now we've gotten so sophisticated with electron microscopes and similar technologies that we're able to map this process out. Each day, we're growing in our understanding of it. It's awe-inspiring, but it still remains something of a mystery.

The most primitive morphogens are positive and negatively charged energies, which are stored in subatomic particles. Peter Mitchell, who was involved in the 1978 Nobel Prize–winning work on cellular energetics, and ionophores, explored the positive and negative charges entering and exiting cell walls that were responsible for cellular energy in the form of ATP. Later it was discovered that subatomic particles and atoms were doing this. Still later, it was discovered that specific amino acids were doing it: these are combinations of elements such as nitrogen, hydrogen, and carbon. Building tissues involves some sort of communication system that works not just in the immediate vicinity, but remotely. So, the nervous system, which operates both electrically and chemically, emerges as an essential way of communicating these little signals to various parts of the body.

I've had dialogues with William Tiller of Stanford University, who has studied subtle energies. We found out that these morphogens activate receptors on the cell wall. These are primarily composed of sugars and proteins, which, being activated, change their shape. This then opens up a gate for the positive and negative charged systems to signal a series of cascading changes in enzymes.

I might also mention the work of biologist Rupert Sheldrake, who has argued that there are fields around the body that influenced these enzymes, which he called *morphogenic fields*. These fields he believed added an almost vitalistic component to this process as well as an electrochemical one. Furthermore, not only can the cells give off micro millivolt fields of life, but the fields can also change the form of simple cellular and more complex multicellular life. Certain experiments used fields to change morphology, which they were evidently able to accomplish. That is, we now know that the fields can alter the genes and the epigenetics.

The Intelligent Universe

Consequently, we can't rule out the possibility that there may be a more subtle field of intelligence that governs life, even though science is still looking at these processes through a mechanistic, materialistic model. Scientists can acknowledge a quantum field theory with excitation of the field manifesting as positively and negatively charged particles or waves and their antiparticles or waves that are synchronously balanced and entangled. Possibly at the more subtle level of Planck-scaled units, there is an intelligence field theory with excitations of the field manifesting as positively and negatively charged emotional memories and their anti-emotional memories or imaginations that are synchronously balanced and entangled.

Soon we will have the first atomic computer, where qubits, spintronics, and even more advanced electronics are able to store information in electrons spinning inside atoms. As we do, we may realize that there is an information base already in existence, and that we're coming in contact with it technologically.

This sounds almost metaphysical, but Leonard Susskind, who is an astrophysicist well respected for his work on string theory derivatives, has suggested that when the information that is absorbed in the stars goes into the black hole, the information is not lost but stored in the throat or walls of the black hole in a two-dimensional grid. Later this information manifests in three dimensions as the black hole gives birth to another system, such as stars or even a whole galaxy. That means that information may be part of the basis of the universe, and we may be adding to it. But we may also be governed by it. We may be living in a participatory holographic universe.

This resembles the debate about whether mathematics is a conceptual mechanism that we have created to deal with chaos or is actually part of nature. I tend to believe it's both: there is mathematics inherent in the universe, but we also make discoveries that eventually approximate the inherent and elegant mathematical truth. We also may have theoretical mathematics that doesn't initially appear to be confirmable or relevant, but later becomes discovered as highly relevant.

I think the same is true with intelligence. I think we're adding to intelligence, but we're also possibly going to discover a more fundamental or underlying ordering intelligence governing the laws of the universe. This may at first appear to be teleological and vitalistic, but this intelligence, which appears to be symmetrically conserved and indestructible, may simply take the form of a mathematical knowledge that we will someday unfold and decipher. There's ever more evidence that this awareness is emerging and developing.

Organogenesis

To go back to ontogeny, the development of the organism, or when organs begin to appear. We go from cells to tissues to organogenesis, the generation of organs. Organs make systems, and systems make the body. Some organs start to develop early and finish early. Some start early and finish late. Others start late and finish early. Still others start late and finish late. And some are finished after we're born.

During this process of organogenesis, let's say you have a congenital anomaly. There are various types of congenital anomalies. Some people can have a horseshoe kidney. Some people can have a C-shaped vertebra in the cervical spine. Typically, when you have one anomaly, you have others, because whatever caused the genetic alteration at a certain phase of organogenesis (such as a systematic toxin or teratogen, or shocking emotion) usually affects other organs that are being formed at the same time. Hence we could have acceleration or retardation at any stage of this organ developing process.

A single cell amoeba selects, engulfs, and absorbs food and removes waste. It seeks and avoids. It has endocytosis for food input and exocytosis for waste removal. Thus, some biologists believe it has a cellular intelligence: it looks for things that are valuable to it and avoids things that aren't. It has a survival impulse for tonic food and an instinct to protect itself from toxic waste. So it possesses a primitive form of cellular intelligence.

If the cellular intelligence occurs in a single-cell organism, then there may also be cellular intelligence at every stage of differentiation. I believe there is; there really is collective intelligences as cells emerge. I believe there's also in a sense a debatable tissue intelligence.

Today's science often has a mechanistic and reductionistic approach rather than a more holistic, vitalistic, or emergent one. Because we don't have an interdisciplinary interaction as much as would be ideal, sometimes we get into partial thinking instead of holistic thinking. By contrast, the lateral thinking of an integrative approach leads to innovations in these fields.

We start out with a single cell (with autocrine or same cell signal communication), then we develop cells that are very close or near to one another (with juxtracrine and paracrine cell signal communication). They influence one another in small spaces and times. As they differentiate, they put systems in place in order to manage complexities and bring order and organization to bigger spaces and times. The nervous system, the endocrine system (with farther cell signal communication), and the circulatory system are designed to accommodate bigger spaces and times within the body.

Similarly, as we evolve and live teleologically, or more purposely, and as we bring our life into fruition, we're continuing to expand our space and time horizons to include our whole selves, our family, our community, our city, our state, our nation, our world, and into space. The magnitude of space and time within our innermost dominant thought determines our level of conscious evolution.

Immediate gratification and reduced space and time horizons regress our physiological and psychological development and diminish our higher order intelligence and organization, which are essential to govern our bodies, resulting in a devolution and our illnesses and physiological and psychological disorders. That is why living by higher priorities adds to eustress and to our wellness quotient.

In his book *Requisite Organization*, Elliott Jaques showed that in corporations, the individual who can manage the greatest domains of space and time has the greatest power. Immediate gratification costs you your life; whereas long-term vision pays off in terms of economics, management, or relationships, and, of course, wellness. If you are living day-to-day in a relationship, it's different than if you have a long-term vision that is moving toward a meaningful or purposeful goal. The key is pursuing and planning out a long-term mission while being present with the highest priority actions in the moment within the plan.

Neuroplasticity

Neuroplasticity is the constant evolving and remodeling of the brain. When I first studied neurology in the latter half of the 1970s, the neurogenesis portion of neuroplasticity was not believed to be frequently happening. It was believed that there was a critical point in development where cellular genesis basically stopped in the brain. Then scientists started finding cells that were undergoing autogenesis and mitotic divisions, neurogenically forming nerves. Now they're finding these processes occurring all over the brain.

When people actively engage or purposely use their brain, they keep their nerves growing. That was at one time not taught and not believed. People were considered uninformed for even thinking such a thing. Now the evidence is so clear that there's no doubt that we have the capacity to pump up our brain as much as we can pump up our muscles. This is magnificent.

Now we're going to look at why and how. The brain is set up with a series of different types of nerves and other cells. I've already mentioned glial cells, which create the framework, you might say the template, around which the neurons build their lives. *Glial* means *neural glue*. Their basic function is to bring nutrition to a nerve, to stimulate it to duplicate itself, to prune it, to eat it if it is dead, to repair it, and to help their synapses strengthen themselves.

There's a variety of glial cells. Most of them, like the nerves, originate embryologically from the neuroblast, but a few of them come from mesenchymal tissue—vascular sources—and are involved in remodeling the brain.

One type is called an oligodendrocyte, because it has little branches that make it look like a tree. When you use your brain, neurons and their myelin sheaths grow. When you don't, they are both eaten. They are pruned, like a tree. Oligodendrocytes bring nutrition and myelin to the nerve cells, but other types of glial cells, the astrocyte and microglia, also prune out the myelin around cells that needs to go.

Then there are microglia consumers and astrocytes supporters, which are specialized cells that come from regions of the vasculature. There are also satellite cells, radial cells, epididymal cells, and Schwann cells. A variety of cells are now classed as glial cells.

Over the last decade, glial cells have become more thoroughly understood and consequently have been recognized as having more significance. They are now regarded as receivers and broadcasting systems of fields and respond to your attention and your intention which are both directed by your highest values. They have a lot of functions. They can impact their surrounding nerves and their accompanying electromagnetic fields.

Researchers have found something really astonishing. The glial cells affect both the sensory and motor, the input and output cells, in the brain. This is where the value system comes in: glial cells respond to your hierarchy of values. We know that the amoeba will redo its structure at a subcellular level to fulfill its aim of survival. Similarly, human beings will remodel their tissues and systems with a homeostatic feedback system in mind to maximally fulfill their mission—their highest value. Your brain or nervous system is a highest-value-seeking organ. It's doing everything it can to help you fulfill what's most meaningful to you, based on what you perceive is most missing and most important. It will both enhance and trim the nervous system for that effect.

Your hierarchy of values dictates your destiny: how you see the world, make decisions in the world, and act upon the world. You have a selective biased attention to whatever is highest on your value hierarchy. I call that ASO: *attention surplus order*. We are highly attentive—there's a surplus attention—and we bring order in our awareness to that which is highest in our values. A mother will not only have a selective biased attention, she'll have a selectively biased *intention*. She will move her muscles to get the things that will benefit her children. She even has a selectively biased *retention*. She will primarily remember things that are going to help her fulfill her highest values. If you talk to her about her children, she'll be more likely to remember everything important to her about them.

When you meet certain people who are valuable to you, you will repeat their names, write them down, and make sure you don't forget them. But if you meet somebody that has zero importance to you, you'll forget their name before they finish saying it. In areas of low value, we have attention deficit disorder as well as *intention* deficit disorder and *retention* deficit disorder. We hesitate and procrastinate. It's not important to us. We don't want our memory to store information that we don't think is going to be useful to us.

Your memory and imagination systems are selected according to the hierarchy of your values. They determine what you love to read, what you want to learn, what you want to absorb, what you want to assimilate, what you allow in, and what you act upon.

When you live congruently according to your highest values, your glial cells help you by myelinating the essential nerve cells that actually fulfill your highest values. Anything that you perceive to be useless toward fulfilling your highest values, they demyelinate, prune, and eat. They neuroplastically restructure your brain to make sure that you fulfill what's most meaningful to you. They help you become resilient.

Fear of Loss, Fear of Gain

There are two primary mechanisms that stop us from adapting: the fear of loss of that which is supporting our hierarchy of values and the fear of gain of that which challenges our hierarchy of values. Let me elaborate on that and tie these themes together.

Would you agree that in your perceptions that some people support and other people challenge you in your life? When somebody supports your set of values, you think of that individual as if they were prey-like, or someone to seek and open up to. When somebody challenges your set of values, you think of that individual as if they were predator-like, or someone to avoid and close down to. You seek prey to eat and they help build you up and are therefore anabolic. You avoid predator so as not to be eaten and they can destroy you and are therefore catabolic.

I've already discussed the parasympathetic and the sympathetic nervous systems, which govern your internal physiology. Whenever you see more support than challenge, your external striated muscles relax, and the blood supply and nutrients go into the internal digestive organs. You digest food, and you go into anabolic activities.

As soon as something challenges you, you move your blood out of the internal digestive organs to the periphery to protect yourself for the purpose of defense. It's like an ancient city with a wall around it. If they're safe and relaxed, they're partying, eating, and feasting in the center of the city. But if all of a sudden somebody challenges or attacks them, they run to the walls and protect their city.

This process also applies at the cellular level. You have the nucleus, and you have the peripheral cell wall, the plasmalemma. When your values are challenged, nutrients are funneled back out to protect the wall. When you feel support and you relax, nutrients go into the nucleus and genes, causing mitosis, growth, and anabolic activities. One is decay and breaking down, and one is growth and building up.

As I've also mentioned, the parasympathetic nervous system is primarily active at night, when you rest and relax. The sympathetic is primarily active during the day, when you're often in fight-or-flight mode because you're tackling the challenges of the day. One process produces mitotic divisions, growth, reduction, and duplication; the other creates apoptosis—cell death, oxidation, and destruction.

If these processes are in perfect equilibrium, you have wellness. If they are out of equilibrium, you have illness. The parasympathetic mode is estrogen based—relaxation and nurture. The sympathetic mode is testosterone based—taking on challenge and being aggressive.

If you pursue fulfilling your highest value, or telos, your whole nervous system will become more objective and balanced and embrace pain and pleasure, support and challenge, equally and resiliently, which leads to wellness. If you attempt to live according to your lower values because you're looking for pleasure, you have an imbalance; you're searching for that which is unattainable and trying to avoid that which is unavoidable. The more you look for immediate consumption, you attract the predator to take advantage of you to keep the equation balanced.

Let's go a step further and take an individual cell. Inside the nucleus, it has DNA, and around the DNA are histones, little protein materials; the two together make up chromatin.

The parasympathetic nervous system primarily deals with acetylcholine. The sympathetic nervous system deals with the tyrosine amino acid derived epinephrine, norepinephrine, and similar substances. These are two primary types of neurotransmitters—cholinergic and adrenergic.

When you perceive more support than challenge, you get one set of transmitters. When you perceive more challenge than support, you get another set. They go to specific locations within the extracellular fluid and lock onto the cell walls, and activate ligand-based receptors, which open up little gates and activate cyclic guanine monophosphate, or cyclic GMP. Or cyclic adenine monophosphate, or cyclic AMP.

This opens up a gate, allowing certain information to get in. As I said, the cell wall is activated or deactivated by little charge particles, which seem to go in and out of the cell wall. That activates a series of enzymes: kinase or phosphatase. Kinase adds phosphate. Phosphatase removes phosphate. Phosphorus is an energy currency. It activates.

The details of these interchanges are extremely complex, but in essence, the same process takes place in the cell that we see in the bodily system as a whole. It's turning on or turning off. It's facilitating and inhibiting. One is growth-oriented, anabolic; one is decay-oriented, catabolic.

When we're living according to our highest values, we have the greatest adaptability or resilience, because we have a balance of the two sides. We're able to embrace both support and challenge equally. When we're attempting to live according to lower values, having clouded our own telos, we feel unfulfilled. We're looking for immediate gratification—consumerism, quick fixes. We become reactive instead of active. We lose our inspiration, and we live quiet lives of desperation, and our autonomic nervous system becomes dominated by the parasympathetic or sympathetic pole, which results in symptoms to let us know it.

In short, living (or not living) according to our telos, our highest values, affects our autonomics, our epigenetics, and our neuroplasticity, which alters our mental function, resulting in some cases in schizophrenia, depression, even epileptic episodes. Autoimmune conditions are becoming more and more rampant. They are self-generated immune responses, which are the result of these imbalanced autonomic and epigenetic effects.

Identifying Emotional Charges

We have what is called a ratio of perception. Sometimes somebody challenges you, but it's not enough to cause a reaction. Other times, they say something that irks you. Still other times, they say something that gets you charged up, and you're ready to fight them.

In the Breakthrough Experience, we ask people to identify somebody that they're emotionally charged about: either someone they highly despise or highly admire. Then we ask them to write down everything they can think of about that individual that they perceive to be negative, that challenges their values, and everything they can think of that they perceive to be positive, that supports their values.

When they perceive the individual to be challenging, they become more resilient when they can also simultaneously perceive the accompanying and supportive upsides to neutralize their perception. But don't forget, resilience is also on the supported side. If you're infatuated with somebody, how fast you can become aware of the simultaneously accompanying and challenging downsides determines how fast you free yourself to go back to being authentic. If you're resenting somebody, and become too proud to own within yourself what you perceive in them and inflate yourself, how fast can you calm yourself back down to authenticity? Your resiliency is determined by the speed at which you can see both sides of an issue, of an individual, that you perceive initially as either good or bad.

If participants are highly resentful of the individual they choose, they're blind to the upsides, and they can easily write many more negatives than positives. What happens if that individual walks into the room? What side is activated? The sympathetic, fight-or-flight side. We get self-righteous and cut them down. We project imperative language onto them: "You should do this; you ought to be that."

But if somebody comes along that we perceived to support our values, we can become highly infatuated. We perceive more positives than negatives and are blind to the downsides.

When you're either infatuated or resentful in regard to these people, you're blind to a portion or half of what is actually going on. That blindness puts you under distress. If you're infatuated, you fear the loss of the individual, or their absence. If you're resentful, you fear the gain of the individual, or their presence. Whenever you have an imbalanced perspective, you're ignoring half of what's there, and we call that ignorance.

Our ignorance reveals itself when we are emotional, reactive, irrational, and fractionated. The more irrational and fractionated we are in our perceptions, the more we activate one of these epigenetic effects to turn our cell functions up and on, or down and off. Illness is excess or deficiency of that cell's normal expression.

If you meet somebody who has just stabbed and raped your child, you'll probably see far more negatives than positives. You might have a negative to positive ratio of seven, or even fifteen or twenty, to one. When you're over a seven to one ratio (either positive to negative or negative to positive), your negative feedback-based intuition is unable to self-regulate and bring you back into homeostatic balance. Then you will probably require assistance as in the case of the Demartini Method being facilitated to return your perceptions back into balance.

But as long as the ratio of positive and negative is within seven to one, you can bring your system back into balance with self-monitoring. Eventually your emotions will calm themselves. If you have a highly emotionally polarized perception of either extreme infatuation or extreme resentment, you exceed the capacity of your intuition to self-govern; you now enter into a bipolar condition or a dissociative almost delusional schizophrenic-like state. Only outside influences, or knowing how to ask the optimal stabilizing questions, will enable to you to reset the thermostat.

Each of the internal and external ecosystems involves a balance of support and challenge. Epigenetics produces symptoms in your body to let you know when you're not perceiving a balance. In the Breakthrough Experience, I ask people specific questions to reveal this balance to them. The moment this happens, they transform their physiology and psychology. Unbelievable changes in health and well-being occur.

As long as we accumulate distorted memories, run those stories, and become victims of our history, we're going to create epigenetic changes and regress. If we have greater than a seven to one ratio at one extreme or the other, we create autonomically polarized seeking or avoiding symptoms to let us know it. When we are so emotionally polarized and distressed over the fear of the loss or gain, we regress our physiology and dedifferentiate the epigenetic gene expression with our cells, reverting back to primitive responses. When we do, we regress back in some of our genetic expressions to the embryological stage, which matches the phylogenetic stage of metazoan one, when single-celled organisms started differentiating into multicellular organisms. At this level, cancers are born. They are initiated when we reactivate ancient, normally dormant genetic toolkits.

The Cause of Cancer

Cancers can be induced by extreme distressing polarities: shocking experiences at some stage of our development process. Anything that reminds us of that experience can keep activating this process. Researchers have found that oncogenes, or viral gene segments that cause cancer, can be turned on or turned off epigenetically. Suppressor genes, which can shut down the genetics for cancer, can also be turned on and off epigenetically.

I have researched this subject for four and half decades. More than what has been acknowledged in oncology influences the development of cancer. Yet very few people in healthcare acknowledge that. They dodge the psychological component, because they know they can't really govern people and people don't govern themselves, and they can't sell that. But people can have extreme emotional stresses that can rapidly initiate and/or promote cancers.

We all have cancer cells constantly emerging and submerging within our body, but they're generally kept under check. We have a surveillance process involving natural killer cells that go around locating and cleaning up cancer cells in our body on a regular basis.

Cancer cells have aneuploidy: imbalanced numbers of chromosome components. Only a small portion of the genes in the genome are actually involved in transcription. The rest of them used to be called junk DNA. Little by little, scientists found out that junk DNA isn't junk. It consists of regulatory components that are reactivated when we're distressed.

Some of those are what are called jumping genes, which transpose their positions, causing expressions similar to genetic mutations, like duplications and deletions. Some of them go forward and transcribe into RNA and proteins or then backward into DNA. They act like viruses inside the cells and can create viral oncogene activation. Our emotions can affect these processes.

Stem cell research can take a skin cell and turn it into a normal heart cell, and vice versa. In a decade, this process will probably be mapped out completely. We'll know how to take a normal cell and take it all the way back to the zygote, and we will be able to differentiate any cell from any other cell. We'll be able to regrow cells to repair tissues. We'll be able to take a skin cell and build a new heart in you that won't be rejected.

When we're in a state of gratitude and love, the forebrain gets blood supply and oxygen. If not, and we're under distress, the blood supply goes into subcortical amygdala and the hindbrain. This means that when we revert to a more subcortical brain function, we can initiate the formation of more dedifferentiated or primitive cellular receptors and signal molecules.

I first discovered this when I was in my twenties. I was looking at the histology, embryology, and pathology texts, and I realized that an amazing correlation was observable. At the time, we didn't have the degree of epigenetic data that we have today. Now I realize that our psychology is inseparable from our physiology. In the future, medicine will be studying not only cells and epigenetics, but the psychological ratios of perception inside the mind that activate and deactivate these pathways, uncovering our potential to transform our own physiology and give rise to wellness or illness.

Quantum Physics and Psychology

In his book *Six Easy Pieces*, Richard Feynman, Nobel Prize winner for quantum electrodynamics, said that there are two types of particles: bosons and fermions.

Bosons are particles of force or energy: the gravitational force, electromagnetic force, the weak nuclear force, and the strong nuclear force.

Fermions are particles of matter and antimatter: positrons, electrons, quarks. The positron and electron communicate with each other through an entangled game via a boson messenger particle called a photon.

A photon is light. It's spaceless, timeless, massless, and chargeless. It's an energy system, but it can be converted into matter and antimatter equivalently according to Einstein's equation. If you take a particle of light, put it in a cloud chamber, you can magnetically separate it into a positron and electron. But they're going to play a game of entanglement with each other. They're going to appear to be separated, although they're not separable in actuality.

When I was eighteen years old and first started studying quantum physics, I wondered, "Is there a metaphorical connection between the human psyche and particle physics?" Various physicists have debated or ignored the possibility and once even said there wasn't. I'm telling you, there is. I demonstrate it in the Breakthrough Experience nearly every week. Today, fifty years later, it is not being ignored. Quantum biology and quantum cognition is emerging.

When you have a positively charged perception of somebody and you think they support your values, and you have somebody that you perceive you resent, that's challenging your values, they're socially entangled. They're actually synchronous, but we're so subjectively biased and ignorant at times that we don't see them simultaneously, because they're not in the same local spatial position and uncertainty reigns. Somebody may be supporting us at work, and somebody may be challenging us at home. If you get pumped up at work, you'll be possibly getting nailed at home. The purpose of a spouse is to get you back in equilibrium. These are spatially and temporally entangled phenomena. With the Demartini Method in the Breakthrough Experience I have assisted thousands of individuals in becoming aware of the synchronicity of these two sides of one macro quantum-like event.

Whenever you become infatuated with someone, you get a dopamine fix, and can become like a juvenile dependent. But you don't grow under juvenile dependency. Moreover, you're blind to the downside. Eventually, you're going to swing to the other side and resent this individual and try to get away from them. You're going to think they're mean and cruel, but actually they're helping you break your addiction-like infatuation with them.

When you're infatuated, you let the animal-like impulse of lust take over, and the subcortical and enteric brain rules you instead of your higher cortical brain, which says, "Hey, there are two sides to this individual. You'd be wise to intuitively know both sides before you mate with them."

If you mate with somebody based on mere immediate gratifying impulse, you'll eventually have an instinct to protect yourself from them when their other opposite side emerges into awareness. But if you moderate the attraction and make sure your intuition and reason bring them into balance, you can love both sides. That's why the marriage ceremony says, "For better or worse, for richer for poorer." If you don't see both sides of the individual, you're going to possibly be lost in infatuation, blind to the downside and eventually broadsided by it. You will activate symptoms in your body to let you eventually know that you were initially impulsive and then later instinctual until your intuition can bring you back into synchronous balance, saying, "Hey, this individual is not who you think." You're ignoring some of the more challenging parts because of your infatuation, but eventually you will discover that they're not who you thought; then you will probably resent them because they didn't match up to your ungoverned fantasy.

You now have symptoms that are trying to get you to intuitively come up with the upsides. It is a homeostatic mechanism to try to get you back to center, where you can love them and yourself equally for both sides. The second you love somebody, and you're no longer either infatuated with them or resentful, you're back to your telos, and you love yourself again. Being around the other individual when you're able to do what you love, living by your highest value, you can have a fulfilling relationship.

A relationship involves identifying the other individual's highest values as well as your own. Ask how their highest values help you fulfill yours. Then, how are your highest values helping them accomplish theirs?

If you can't answer those questions, you're going to live with alternating monologues rather than a meaningful and respectful dialogue. You're going to create miscommunication drama, or you're going to create symptoms, disease, to let you know that you're not loving and living true to yourself. You're distracted by an illusion of them and yourself. Your epigenetics will give you feedback to get you back to real love, where you embrace support and challenge or pleasure and pain together in the pursuit of your most meaningful purpose. It is here that you maximize your resilience of mind.

Telos and Life-Span

The genes are capped by telomeres: the ends of the genes. The end of the brain is called the telencephalon: the forebrain.

When you live according to your highest value–based telos, you activate the telencephalon, and you extend the telomeres. But when you're distressed and isolated and don't see yourself reflected in people around you—as both hero and villain—you shorten the telomeres. Your blood goes into your amygdala and hindbrain with distress, and you shorten your life-span, because the further back you go, the shorter your space and time horizons, and your space and time horizons will impact how broad and well your cells interact and how long you live.

The lower the socioeconomic level, generally the lower the space and time horizons. The factory worker lives day to day. The supervisor lives week to week. Lower management, month to month. Middle management, year to year. Upper management, decade to decade, and the CEO may think in terms of a generation. Visionaries may think in terms of a century. Sages may think in terms of a millennium. The soul is thinking in terms of eternity. As Seneca implied, you measure an individual by their most distant ends.

The magnitude of space and time within individuals' innermost dominant thoughts determines their level of conscious evolution. At a higher socioeconomic level, people tend to have a lower fertility and lower mortality rate. At a lower level, they tend to have a higher fertility and higher mortality rate. The fertility and mortality rates are inversely proportional to the magnitude of space and time in their innermost dominant thoughts.

A company's fertility and mortality rate will be based inversely on the size and magnitude of its leader's vision. If they're living day to day, they're not as likely to make it. If they have a great and inspiring enough vision to endure the distractions of transient pleasures and pains in pursuit of that vision, they will endure.

Immediate gratification can cost you your life, just as it can cost you your money. People who receive money and spend it immediately and in a manner beyond their means will be working their whole lives as slaves for money. They will probably even end up at a lower socioeconomic level and with shorter life-spans because wealth is one factor in longevity. The more wealth you have, the longer you will be likely to live. The higher the socioeconomic level, the higher the level of education you probably have also had. More education means that you have probably taken on a greater concentric sphere of space and time in your awareness. And you have probably taken on or contributed to taking on greater humanitarian challenges.

If you're not taking on and solving individual or social challenges, you're possibly not fully living and may even be slowly dying. Empowered, alive, and resilient individuals pursue challenges that inspired them. If there's no meaningful challenge, there's no growth. An authentic and fulfilling life requires ever greater challenges as much as support.

Factors in Longevity

One factor in longevity is knowing your highest values and prioritizing your daily actions to do what's most meaningful and inspiring to you—also giving yourself permission to do something extraordinary on planet Earth—some inspired action that truly serves.

Next is drinking a lot of water. Water is the most universal solvent. It helps keeps the essential redox (reduction-oxidization) biochemical or metabolic systems in order. Excessive stimulants or sedatives can cause volatility. The more volatility, the shorter the probable life-span. People who attempt to live according to their lower values, who function from their more animal-like and passionate amygdala tend to narrow their minds and experience more volatility. Someone living according to their higher values will tend to rise to a higher contribution level. They function from their higher brain center, or guardian angel, and tend to expand their mission as they reach up and out into the celestial spheres with their broader vision, not in the narrower terrestrial spheres, living day to day. This greater view and vision helps extend their life and adds to their resilience.

Another key is your breathing. When you are perceptually challenged, your sympathetic system is activated, and you tend to have longer inhalations and shorter exhalations. When you are perceptually supported, your parasympathetic is activated, and you tend to have longer exhalations and shorter inhalations. In either case you have imbalanced breathing. As the yogis used to say, as the mind wanders, so does the breath. As the breath wanders, so does the mind. If the mind is not balanced, the breath will not be balanced. The more balanced your breath, the longer your life, because your breath is your life. Your life starts with the first breath and ends with the last. If you don't know how to moderate your breathing, you shorten your life-span.

Volatilities in breathing will shorten life-spans. They won't even let children out of a hospital if their breathing processes are too shallow and volatile. Breathing deeply and diaphragmatically, in a one-to-one ratio of inhalations and exhalations, drinking lots of water, moderating excessive stimulants and sedatives, limiting sugars, eating quality food, and living according to your telos are essential for a long and fulfilling life.

Make sure that you get outdoors in nature and walk, using, stretching, and lubricating all your joints and muscles. Whenever you activate the parasympathetic system, it activates your flexors, pronators, and adductors. Your sympathetic system will activate your extensors, your supinators, and abductors. Whenever there's a conflict between the two autonomic systems, there's tension between those agonist and antagonist muscles, and there's no congruency, fluidity, and grace in their function. This results in abnormal tensions and compressions in the joints and tissues, which then leads to degeneration of bones, abnormal pressures on joints, and degenerative joint diseases. It creates an imbalance in piezoelectrical tension or pressure, or positive and negative electrical charges that alter cells and can even in some cases activate cancers.

Theology and the Universe

The theological constructs within global humanity reflect a gradation of awareness. In the earliest more primitive stages, we were frightened of many things in nature that challenged us, so we made up gods to appeal to who some believed would suppress, protect, and override it. We would create a god or heroic deity in the image of anything that would conquer our anxieties.

Eventually, as our brains expanded and developed, we understood the challenges within nature more rationally. Now it wasn't the weather, the earth, the plants, or the animals within nature that frightened us; it was other human beings. So we created gods in our own image. We created anthropomorphic deities and made them omnipresent, omniscient, and omnipotent.

Beyond all these, there's the potential intelligence of the universe, which transcends the anthropomorphisms: it has no form, race, creed, color, age, or sex; it constantly manifests in a balance between support and challenge, building and destroying. In physics, we call it the laws of conservation and the laws of symmetry and it expresses a mathematical elegance. These laws are what Albert Einstein was talking about when he spoke of true religiosity. The rest are sometimes transient anthropomorphic fantasies.

Divine comes from roots meaning to *emanate*, to *shine*. Divine intelligence may just turn out to be what quantum theorists are describing as the quantum vacuum with its emerging and submerging particles of light and charged particles of matter and antimatter, which some believe originates the so-called big bang. True science and religion aren't fighting, but anthropomorphic deity-based religions and some atheistic scientists, who oppose those religions, tend to fight. The true scientists are humble in their awareness and willing to live in the mysteries, not just the limited histories, and ask the truly greater questions. At the same time, they're often frightened of metaphysical questions, because the answers are at first speculative. We have no way of pinning them all down, although each generation pins down a little bit more.

There just may be an intelligence in the universe, a conserved and magnificent underlying information-based order and we're all part of it. No matter what you do, you're in a living social matrix of support and challenge. Most of us live with subjective evaluations and illusions. We think things are separated when they're actually entangled in synchronicities in ways we don't usually see. When you see them, you're brought to inspired tears of gratitude for the order that's here. It is a synthesis and synchronicity of all complementary opposites. It transcends the infatuations that most people equate with love, and it's helping us grow and evolve intelligently out into ever greater domains of space and time and beyond, into the vast and mysterious present, because that appears to be our destiny.

Chapter 5

Life's Hard Knocks

Resilience has a great deal to do with managing the hard knocks in life. They are feedback mechanisms, trying to get you back to living by your telos and embracing both sides of life. Maximum growth and development occur at the border of support and challenge.

There are two forms of distress: the perception of loss of what we seek, and the perception of gain of what we avoid. If you make a list of any distress you'll ever have in your life, you'll find it boils down to one of those two forms. For instance, if you're seeking money, the perception of loss of money can be distressful, but so is the perception of gain of things that can take it away, such as bills or thieves.

As I've already discussed, distress is a feedback mechanism to let you know you're not living by your highest value. Infatuations can occupy space and time in your mind and can distract you. The same is true of resentments. But if you're in a balanced state of love for life, you're not distracted: your energy is used to fuel genius, innovation, and creativity, and it is here that you become most resilient.

Wide River

Early in the 1990s, I was on a flight to California. Next to me was a quiet man whose energy seemed to be drained, and a bit distraught, and we started a conversation.

"What do you do?" I asked.

"I'm in the music industry."

"Fantastic. Do you write music?"

"I have."

"What type?"

"It's an older genre, it's a more rock and roll type, but I've been in a slump for a while. I haven't done much exceptionally creative lately. I haven't come up with any new songs."

I started thinking that I might be able to help him. "You know," I said, "there's a methodical step-by-step technique that you can do to get your creative genius flowing again. Do you mind if I have some fun with you?"

"No, fine."

I learned that he was preoccupied by the passing of someone he knew. He was also not fully appreciating himself because he hadn't created any new music and his band recognition was fading a bit. He hadn't done anything that he considered as great recently, and he was living on his past fame.

I started to use a questioning process that I had developed of clearing his bereavement grief. I dissolved his grief through a series of questions, and he had a tear of gratitude instead of a tear of sorrow over his initially assumed loss. Then I had him go through and think about what else he was grateful for. I also helped him reframe anything he was having difficulty being grateful for and see it from a different perspective by using the Demartini Method. All of a sudden, he came out of his slump and livened up.

"All right now," I said, "close your eyes, go inside, and think about what you are now grateful for. Don't stop until you get a tear of appreciation and inspiration in your eye. The second you do, I'll see it. Then we're going to go inward, and allow some inspired lyrics to be revealed and come up with a new song."

It took him a moment to reflect on what he was grateful for, and suddenly he broke through and reached his gratitude threshold, and a tear came to his eye. When he did, and some music and lyrics came through. He had to write them down.

As he was thinking about the song, his body was moving, and then he leaned back in his chair. I didn't know it, but four of his band members were in a row behind us. He leaned over and started singing his new lyrics, and they started singing and playing it in their heads. They created a song called "Wide River."

It was rock star Steve Miller. I didn't know who he was at first. I said, "I listened to your bands back in the freaking seventies and eighties, man."

"Yeah, I know. We've been kind of dry lately."

Later I saw him interviewed on a show, and he was asked how this song had come to be written.

"I was flying on a plane," he said, "and this guy was sitting next to me. And he was doing some weird stuff, and out came my song." I thought that was hilarious.

Sometimes when you're thinking there is a challenge, if you ask the optimal questions and perceive it differently and decide to see it as *on* the way, not *in* the way, that crisis becomes your greatest blessing. Steve Miller might not have had one of his great songs if he hadn't had that moment of reflection and inspiration. The crisis is the blessing.

The Search for Life

Once I was a guest speaker for the Waldzell Conference at the Melk Abbey in Austria, overlooking the Danube—a beautiful place. Another speaker was geneticist and cell biologist Paul Nurse, who won a Nobel Prize for his work on how the eukaryotic cell cycle is controlled and how cell shape and cell dimensions are determined. When he won, the committee told him they needed a completed and authenticated biography of his life to put in their annals.

Nurse started doing some homework and discovered something he didn't know, even though he was in his fifties. He found that his mother and father weren't his mother and father. The people he thought were his mother and father turned out to be his grandparents. He had what he thought was an older sister who had gotten pregnant as a young teenager. The parents were a bit humbled; they could not allow her to be seen that way, so they shipped her to another city away from the family. She carried the baby to term, and after the baby was born, her parents took the baby boy and raised him.

So this little boy grew up with possibly an innate yearning to know its origin and development of life and its true genetic code. He had a need to know these things enough to pursue this knowledge for decades—information that nobody had ever figured out before. He got the Nobel Prize for it.

When Nurse was awarded the prize in Stockholm, he wanted to acknowledge his sister/mother. She had been isolated, but if it wasn't for her and his grandparents' actions, he probably wouldn't have this prize. The family had gone from the greatest shame to the greatest fame and the greatest appreciation in the family. The family crisis they had thought was a setback brought about one of the most profound moments of their lives.

We don't always see this balance initially. But by asking the optimal questions and finding the blessing within the crisis, the master sees and embraces both sides. The majority of people try to escape half of their lives, searching for an opium, a one-sided fantasy. They suffer reversals that they blame on the outside, then look for something on the outside to save them. They don't realize that everything on the outside reflects what's on the inside; there's nothing missing inside us.

Meeting Paul Nurse was an inspiring moment. He said that he could not get out of his mind the yearning to know the origin and development of life and the genetic code. Deep inside, he knew without knowing that there was a mystery in his life that hadn't been solved yet.

When I was a child, my foot, leg, and arm were turned in, and I had to wear metal and leather braces. I begged my dad to let me out of them at age four, but he told me if he did I would have to keep my leg and arm straight, otherwise I would return to the braces. All I wanted to do was to be free and run, and I've been independent and on the run ever since.

When I was a very young child, I was also taken to a speech pathologist. When I was age six and began first grade I was told by my teacher—in front of my parents—that I would probably never be able to read, write, or communicate, never amount to anything, never go very far in life. That was perfect, because that was exactly the void I needed to do what I'm doing today. If you haven't seen your many possibly perceived obstacles as *on* the way rather than *in* the way, you haven't looked deeply enough to discover the higher order to your apparent chaos. It may now be time to look again.

Curing Multiple Sclerosis

Once I was in Sydney, Australia, doing a five-day presentation on nearly 1,000 health conditions—neuroendocrinology, psychology, and physiology. I wrote a textbook on these conditions discussing the psychological, autonomic, and epigenetic reasons why we end up with these illnesses. It's kind of a mind-body compendium.

For five days, the students and I were exploring condition after condition, looking at how the autonomic nervous system, with its neurotransmitter, and secondary epigenetic impact, affects the expression or repression of genes, alters proteins, and causes changes in cellular function. We correlated those variables with perceptions of events that occur in our life to see how our minds and bodies create symptoms.

We went right through the systems of the body and nearly 1,000 different types of conditions. When we got to multiple sclerosis—MS—a gentleman put his hand up and said, "Dr. Demartini, do you mind if I ask a question about MS? I have MS, and I've been told that it's just a matter of weeks before I'm going to have to live in a wheelchair. My left arm is very weak; I can barely move it. I'm not able to put weight on my left leg anymore, and my left eye is pretty well out of function due to optic neuritis. Frankly, it more than scares me. What might have led to this? Is there anything I might be able to do about it?"

"I don't know without asking you some questions," I said. "I was mainly just educating." But I thought, "Let's see what I might be able to do for him."

I went over and asked him about some history, because the history reveals a lot. He was in a job that he was unfulfilled in. He saw no light at the end of the tunnel and didn't know if he could handle it any longer. But he was making and saving enough that he figured if he could just get to a certain amount, he would have enough of a cushion to start doing something he wanted to do. He hadn't really delineated the new career path clearly, but he felt if he could just get a breather, it would be great. He'd save enough money to get to that point, and he was counting the days until he had this amount.

The day he decided, "I'm now able to be free; I'm going to finally quit this job," he went home to tell his then partner and mother, only to find out that they both required additional financial assistance. The idea that he had this added responsibility made him freeze inside, and he couldn't say what he wanted to say. In that moment he was angry, but he judged himself because of the injected values of society: how can you be angry at your partner and mother for needing help?

This gentleman had an internal conflict between what he wanted to do and what he felt he had to do now. His vision was gone. He lost grasp. He lost his footing—on the left side of his body, the female side. Within days, he got tingling, numbing, and weakness; the symptoms of MS were beginning. He was screaming inside, and he felt trapped, but he couldn't say so because he felt he shouldn't. And he said, "I'm trapped in this frigging job."

I used the Demartini Method to help him see things from a different perspective and find the hidden order in the apparent chaos. We worked through what had happened and how his illness was trying to make sure he received attention and he got what he wanted. Now he had a reason to get out of his job, with insurance to cover him. That was his only escape. Illness is often the result of unconscious strategies.

While we were working and sorting through his unconscious motives and strategies, his eyes suddenly teared up, his nose dripped, and his mouth drooled from a deep realization. His girlfriend put her arm around him, and he went through a catharsis for fifteen minutes there in the seminar.

Finally, he saw some light at the end of the tunnel—why he created his illness—and he saw what he really wanted to do: help people to keep from being trapped. That was his dream, to help people get past their traps, and he saw a way to do it.

After the seminar, this gentleman went home and slept more soundly that night. The next morning, he got up, was driven to the seminar venue, entered the seminar room, and came right up to me. I was getting my mic on, preparing to speak. He put his arms around me and said, "I can see you with my left eye. I can hold you with my left arm. And I walked up the steps by myself, with my left leg. Whatever happened yesterday, something changed."

"Fantastic. With MS, sometimes you have remissions and exacerbations: it goes up and down, so you can't state if this is more than a temporary condition, but let's keep working."

That afternoon, when I left to fly out, this gentleman went with me to the airport. In the club lounge, we laid out a plan of action, using the Demartini Method to dissolve every single issue we could identify in order to expedite his healing process.

This gentleman went to work. He did not do it just partly. He dissolved every subconsciously stored internal conflict and judgment that he could identify in his life—resentments, challenges, and things he wasn't grateful for. He made a list of them, and he went through methodically, using the Demartini Method to clear them out.

His neurologist said, "Don't get your hopes up; this is temporary; this is a progressive degenerative disease."

Six months later, the neurologist said, "Something has definitely happened. We haven't had any symptoms, and usually in six months some symptoms would have again happened."

This gentleman said, "I've just come back from the Demartini Method training program. Do you mind if I work with some of your other MS patients, just in case there's something I can do?" He started working with other MS patients, clearing out the baggage, and started getting similar results. Years later, this man can jog; he has no signs of MS today.

I don't know what the limits of the human body are, but I do know that our symptoms are trying to get us back to authenticity. If we uncover the message and the mission that it's revealing, it guides us to do something extraordinary, because the power within us is far greater than the obstacles around us. The symptoms are trying to make us resilient and authentic.

This gentleman's previous crisis is now his blessing. He is inspired by what he's doing today. He's making great money doing this method on people. He's helped dozens of people with MS now and is transforming some neurologist's viewpoints.

The crisis is the blessing. The hard knocks are the gift. The setback is the step forward; the scar is the star. Let's take the time to look deeper. Whenever we fill our minds and days with our highest-priority actions, we expand our resiliency, adaptation, and ability to see and embrace both sides, ourselves, and the world around us.

An Eleven-Year-Old Designer

Another time I was speaking at a conference in Las Vegas, and an eleven-year-old girl named Hanalei Swan came up on stage to present an inspiring speech. After her presentation I asked her, "What's the biggest challenge that you've turned into an incredible opportunity?"

"When I was born," she said, "my parents lost everything and filed for bankruptcy. They read *The 4-Hour Workweek* and decided, 'Let's leave everything and start traveling.' That was my biggest win. It helped me become who I am today, because I got to see the world for what it truly is instead of reading about it in a textbook. I was able to find inspiration from different cultures, peoples, and places around the world. During my travels I began creating fashionable clothing designs, and I kept my ideas in a sketchbook.

"One time we were in Bali. We were sitting in a restaurant next to a woman who was talking with my parents. I was fast asleep on the couch seat in the restaurant.

"My mom asked the woman, 'What do you do for a living?'

"'I'm a fashion designer.'

"Out of nowhere I woke up. I had my sketchbook right next to me, and I said, 'I am too.'

"'If you're a fashion designer, you must have your sketchbook with you,' said the woman.

"I showed her. She looked at my sketches and said, 'These need to be made into reality.'

"Since then," the girl said, "I've been a fashion designer. That gave me the inspiration to find out and do what I love. I decided I wanted to make amazing designs to make women feel beautiful." At that time she had six employees working for her.

"But," she went on, "as I've traveled and revisited places, I have seen so much pollution on our earth. Some places that were once beautiful are now full of trash. I combined my mission of saving the planet with my love of art and fashion. Now I'm able to do what I love every day and help our earth."

Can you see that this family's crisis became their blessing? The bankruptcy may have seemed like the most challenging event at the time, but it had within it something supportive and gave birth to something inspiring.

Teaching and Values

I'm often approached by parents who say, "I'm concerned about my son's schooling experience. My son is very depressed. He's being taught topics which are definitely not perceptually aligned with his higher intrinsic values and actions. He's bored. He hasn't had an opportunity to study or do what he would truly love to do from a young age. He's been pushed through a system that he is perceiving as incongruent with his highest values and ideals."

Occasionally I speak in schools, to teachers, principals, and students. I've yet to meet a boy or girl regardless of age that didn't love learning, but they want to learn what is most intrinsically meaningful and inspiring to them. I think it's quite unfair for any child to go to any class without knowing why and how that class will help them fulfill what is most meaningful to their life.

When I go to the school, I sit with the teachers, and we identify their highest values. I have the Demartini Value Determination process: it's on my website, drdemartini .com, and it's free and private. Please take a moment to fill it out. It'll take thirty minutes of your time. Do it a few times, because we tend to lie to ourselves initially. We tend to write what we wish our values would be or what they used to be instead of writing down objectively what our life demonstrates or reveals. Keep doing that question-based survey until you can look at it and say, "I've got it; that's what my life truly demonstrates is most valuable."

Once I determine the teacher's values, I take their classes and ask, "How is teaching this particular class, topics and subtopics going to help you fulfill what's most meaningful and important to you as a teacher?" If they can't see how that class is going to help them fulfill what's meaningful to them, they're not going to be engaged. They won't keep current with cutting-edge information. They won't be enthused or inspired. They'll be boring, and no one's going to want to sit and listen through their presentations and lessons.

So for three hours, I have the teachers link each class they have with their highest values, so they can see that the class is deeply meaningful in helping them achieve what is truly most important to them—their highest values. I've done this with a lot of teachers, and they're completely different when they go into class the next time. Because they're now seeing their teaching curriculum as *on* the way, not *in* the way. They're not teaching because they have to, because those are the rules. They're doing it because they now can see that this is going to be deeply meaningful to them. This takes about four hours in total.

Next I go to the students on the first day of class, and I help them determine their highest values in the same way. I have them ask how specifically the classes they are about to take are going to help them fulfill what they value most. We work as a group and help everybody find out how these classes are going to serve them. When the students walk in, they start out saying, "They're not, man; they're useless and antiquated. What am I going to do with this information? I have no idea."

If students can't see how their classes are going to help them fulfill or achieve where they would love to go, they won't want to take them. They become bored or uninspired. They're then labeled as having attention deficit disorder and put on medication. But at home they can sit for six hours and play video games, or socialize, or play a sport. They don't have an attention deficit in the area they are inspired by most. They have it in a class that's not inspiring, taught by a teacher who's not inspiring, with a curriculum that's meant for drones, not leaders, that they cannot relate to and is perceived as disengaging.

As long as students have that attitude, why would they ever want to go to class? Why would they want to remember what they learned? They have no engagement whatsoever, but in my linking sessions, they learn how that class is going to help them get what they want.

In my signature seminar program, the Breakthrough Experience, I teach people this same skill: how to take anything in their life and see how it helps them get what they want. That is worth an unbelievable amount, particularly to those feeling disengaged in life. Most people are living quiet lives of desperation because they don't know how to do it.

Once we've taken the students and shown them the links, they won't be going to class for the sake of the class; they'll be going because they want to learn and fulfill their highest values. Nobody merely wants to learn something; they want to learn something that's meaningful and most important to them.

With some classes, students do really well. But, for the classes they're having the most difficulty with, you can simply ask them how taking this class will help them fulfill what they truly want in life. I guarantee that every class can be linked. I've yet to see a class that's unlinkable to any highest value that a child has. They just don't know it. It is simply being persistent and holding them accountable to keep looking. With every new link made in their minds between the class or topic and their highest values, the greater their learning engagement and the more resilient they become.

Delegating

A woman attending one of my seminars in London a few years ago approached me with this statement and question: "I went through some very transformative tragedies in my life. I lost three members of my family. I lost my home, and recently I've come out of a ten-year relationship. I am financially challenged at the moment and finding life incredibly difficult. You have spoken about delegating low-priority tasks, but when you are financially challenged, how on earth can you delegate?

"Because of these perceived tragedies, I ended up following a new career path which I certainly do love, but it's not yet making me enough money to survive. I run singing clubs in the UK and in different cities in Europe. I run them in schools, and I work with underprivileged people and people who have learning difficulties. Through them I've helped people out of depression, but it barely makes enough for me to survive alone in London. I can't afford to delegate. I can't pay people to help me."

In response to this woman's statement and question, I told her that the purpose of delegation is to free you up to do what's higher on your list of priorities and what can potentially produce a greater amount of service and income. If you're not doing some form of service that's truly meeting others' needs enough for them to desire to pay you a fair exchange and which produces more than the cost of delegation, you won't be able to delegate. So delegation is not an abnegation. It is for the purpose of you having the freedom to do actions that are higher in value, more productive and more financially viable.

If you feel unworthy of receiving greater financial income or great wealth for what you're doing, you may want to look at what you feel ashamed about or guilty of in the past, because past shame and guilt can create altruistic behaviors to compensate—to feel greater about ourselves by rescuing people that represent parts of us we haven't loved.

Try giving yourself permission to serve people while valuing yourself and packaging your service in a way that people will pay for. That way, you maintain a sustainable fair exchange; you have the income to be able to delegate so you'll be able to serve ever more people.

If you're poor, it just may be because you're not caring enough about contributing to humanity. If you did, you would find a way of serving humanity directly or indirectly with a product, service, or idea. Instead of focusing on you, you focus on the service and on making a difference in their lives. You'll get paid if it serves a true need. "So," I told this woman, "I would encourage you to prioritize: what is the highest-priority service you can do and stick to the one that produces the most income? This means you are truly serving others. By doing that, you can delegate the other lower priority action steps and be able to do your philanthropic work too.

"If you've never thought about how you could produce substantial income while providing your service, I would encourage you to get clear about how to do that. How do you serve ever greater numbers of people and get handsomely paid to do it? It's just a matter of asking the optimal question and being accountable enough to create or discover the answer.

"You are probably holding on to some shame or guilt in the past that makes you feel you have to do something altruistic, and it's blocking you from comfortably receiving a sustainable and then profitable income. My Demartini

Method includes processes that can efficiently clear that shame and guilt and allow you to receive. Many people cannot get over this threshold economically until that occurs. But I have a feeling there's a little bit of shame or guilt lingering in your mind. I don't know if that answers your question, but let's decide exactly what you would love to do and package it in a way that it's actually making the income you would love. You won't convince me it can't be done. It's just a matter of brainstorming, asking the essential questions, and applying strategic action steps."

Chapter 6
Dealing with Depression

One mental health issue that I frequently come across is depression. You have probably had moments when you've had lows, if not an actual genuine clinical depression. Although there are different criteria for defining or determining a clinical depression, today's pharmaceutically driven psychiatrists commonly believe that you have a biochemical imbalance and you need medication. This belief has been significantly challenged by recent long-term research.

I'm not saying that doesn't occur at times, but I feel certain that it's not as often as has been promoted and believed. People look for a pill for every illness, for a quick fix, instead of taking command of their lives and learning what's underlying the depression and what they can do about it.

Suppose you came up to me and said that you're depressed. Your psychiatrist said you have a biochemical imbalance, and you need medication. You believe that because you've been told that it's a biochemical imbalance, there's nothing you can do; you have to take medication for it.

But suppose I said, "Behind this door, there's a giant tiger. I'm going to open the door, and I'm going to let the tiger into the room you are in. He wants to eat you. He's going to leap across the room directly toward you, and his mouth is going to be open, with fangs and saliva. Just as it's about to grab your face and head, I'm going to freeze-frame everything, so the tiger's in midair, with his mouth open and salivating over your head. I'm going to quickly go in and do a blood analysis of your brain chemistry. Guess what I'll find? You'll not have a normal blood chemistry. It will be significantly changed due to the distressful perception of a predator about to eat you.

"Within a billionth of a second, your chemistry changed. Your dopamine, serotonin, endorphin, enkephalin, vasopressin, oxytocin, and estrogen immediately dropped. Your testosterone rapidly went up. So did your histamine, osteocalcin, cortisol, norepinephrine, and epinephrine. Your substance P went up. The pain and fight-or-flight chemistry went rapidly up.

"You're going to have a biochemical imbalance, and it's going to occur in a millisecond. Your perceptions come in at the speed of electrical conduction, changing the hormones in the hypothalamus and the neurohormones and neurotransmitters in the autonomic nervous system.

"Now all of a sudden the tiger comes down, and stands and puts his arms around you, and says, 'I'm Tony the

Tiger, and you're grrrreat!' You've always loved Tony the Tiger because you ate Frosted Flakes cereal as a child. You think, 'Oh, my God, I finally met Tony the Tiger!' He hugs you and wants to take a picture with you. Now you're having a grand time with Tony the Tiger.

"If I freeze-frame this scene and evaluated your blood neurochemistry, guess what we would find? Your dopamine, oxytocin, and vasopressin would have gone up. There are desire and bonding compounds that rise. Up go the estrogen, serotonin, enkephalins, and endorphins, while the other chemistries that I just mentioned—cortisol, epinephrine, and histamine—go down. You've flipped, just like that.

"If I froze this scene, your psychiatrist would say you have a biochemical imbalance, but the psychiatrist didn't tell you that your biochemical imbalance had a lot to do with your present and previous subconsciously stored perceptions."

You may say, "I don't have those extreme perceptions, and I'm still depressed." Maybe you do, and maybe you don't know it.

Neurosocial Complexes

Let me give you another scenario. Say you're at home on a Sunday, and you've decided to take an easy day. Then you get in a fight with your spouse, and you really have a yelling match with each other.

Right in the middle of the fight, the doorbell rings. You repress your momentary anger and go over to the door and see your friends, who say, "We're in the neighborhood; we thought we'd drop by."

"Come on in," you say, and you put on a smile, covering up what you're really feeling.

You have a two-hour conversation with your friends. You have a nice time with them, but you still have a festering relationship issue sitting inside your mind, temporarily buried. Then your friends leave. You really haven't cleared the air. Your spouse goes about his or her business quietly, and you go about yours. You have a subtle frustration that you don't resolve.

You go to work the next day, and your spouse goes and does what he or she does. The issue fizzles out but is not resolved. Sometimes something reminds you of it, and up come those repressed emotions again.

These emotions are stored in the brain's electronics and chemistry, what they call the neuro associated complexes, or engrams, which are now electronically imbalanced. We store those imbalances as noise or static in the brain. When you're either infatuated or resentful, or proud or shamed, you have noise in the brain: you can't get the other individual or yourself out of your mind; they or you are occupying your mind, and it's hard to sleep.

This perceptually induced biochemical imbalance hasn't just occurred because the brain automatically goes haywire one day. It's because you've accumulated many of these emotionally polarized subconsciously stored judgment splits or perceptual imbalances. They're running your chemistries even though you're not aware of it and nobody's telling you about it.

You may not be skilled at knowing how to peel back the onion and get to these stored emotions or how to regress yourself back to those moments and clear them. You may not have the tools, so the only solution is a pharmaceutical pill. I'm not saying it doesn't have a place; it does. In some cases, there are genetic defects in the brain, or injuries. You may have some reason why your brain is imbalanced, but I see that extremely rarely. I'd rather empower people and show them how they can reduce or reverse their accumulating subconscious infatuations or resentments and learn how to master their lives. That's what I want to present now.

What Depression Is

I want to share with you an alternative perspective on what depression is in my terms and talk about a few of the people I've been able to work with. I've worked with thousands of people who are supposedly depressed, at least they are diagnosed with that, and I've found something quite unique.

I'd rather show you how to dissolve those issues so that you can possibly reduce or eliminate the need for pills. I've had a lot of people in my programs that have been diagnosed clinically depressed but are no longer depressed or taking medication. I haven't taken them off: they've taken themselves off, sometimes with their doctors, sometimes without. Not because I've told them to; they just no longer seem to have a need for them. They know how to balance their minds and take command of their brain's neurochemistry.

With that said, let me discuss what you might do if you feel you might be or are depressed. Let me explain what I define depression to be.

I've already discussed the hierarchy of values, or the values structure. You become more objective and neutral in your perceptions when you begin living by priority in accordance with your highest values. And you awaken your self-governing prefrontal cortical executive center. As stated previously, objectivity also means even-mindedness: you're more balanced in mind and therefore more balanced in your neurochemistry. When you're living congruently with your highest values, you embrace both the positives and the negatives in life more equitably. But when you attempt to live according to your lower values, like when you compare yourself to others and look up to them and then attempt to live in their values and not your own highest values, you tend to become more subjective, that is, un-even-minded. When you're down at that level, you have a higher probability of being volatile and filled with survival-based emotions, because you are unfulfilled and your amygdala begins to come online.

Again, let's take the example of the little boy who loves video games. If you're this boy, you'll work day and night on your game. You don't need to be reminded to do it. The second you conquer it, you go to your parents to get a more challenging game. You're not shrinking from challenges; you're looking forward to tackling them to see what you're capable of doing.

That's how you behave when you're living by your highest values: you embrace challenges that help you fulfill what you dream about. You're able to appreciate the support and the challenge equally; therefore, you're more balanced, resilient, adaptable, and capable in that area. Whenever you set goals that align with your highest value, you're more balanced; you're less likely to be volatile or emotional and less manic and depressed. People who live by their highest values, in their executive center, don't have as many extreme emotional swings, unlike people who live in the lower values and become trapped in their amygdala responses and become volatile.

How and why do we transiently attempt to live in our lower values? Very simple. Have you ever met somebody that you thought had a greater life than you? Have you compared yourself to them, thinking they were smarter, wealthier, or more successful or influential than you—or for that matter, more spiritually aware? In the comparison, you felt small, fatigued, and kind of down.

That's because you're comparing your current reality to a fantasy of being them and not you. They may not in fact be what you think, but you assume they are. When you try to be more like them, you inject their values into your life and try to live in these values instead of your own. Whenever you try to live in other people's values, you're almost guaranteed to devalue yourself through such comparison. You go into a more primitive part of the brain, the amygdala, and function more subjectively. You're more likely to be impulsive and instinctive, seeking prey or positives, avoiding predators or negatives. Bipolar condition is a byproduct of monopolar addiction and subdiction.

Now why am I saying this? Because a lot of depression goes with bipolar swings. That means cycles of mania and depression. Depression is a comparison of your current reality to a fantasy about how you want your life to be. You're in a sense dopamine addicted to that fantasy, and you don't want to lose it. Because you're attempting to live in your lower values, in the amygdala, you're unfulfilled. As compensation, you seek immediate gratification—a quick fix.

Addictive behavior and a desire for one-sidedness, for happiness without sadness, pleasure without pain, ease without difficulty, pride without shame, the positive without the negative, are by-products of unfulfilled highest values. When you're doing something you love, you're more balanced, or objective, stable, inspired, and grateful. You embrace pain and pleasure in pursuit of what is more meaningful and purposeful, and you're more resilient.

If you're not fulfilling your highest values because you're comparing yourself to others, injecting their values into your own, and trying to be somebody else, you'll lose yourself. You're going to deprecate yourself, and you're going to look for a quick fix as a dissociative-associative compensation.

Depression is a comparison of your current reality to a fantasy about what you want that isn't even exactly true. As long as you're holding on to a fantasy, your life's going to be a nightmare. Yet the way life really is—balanced—is more magnificent than any fantasy.

Depression is a low that occurs as a result of an addiction to a high. Anything that you think is going to give you a positive that is greater than a negative will, when you find out that it's balanced, lead to a negative that is greater than a positive. Whenever you're not filling your day with high-priority actions, you're more vulnerable to both manic and depressive states. You go back and forth. Searching for an unobtainable one-sided world will be futile and certainly depressing.

Unfulfilled people are more affected by things on the outside, because they're driven by outside rewards and punishments instead of an inside poise. People who are driven by the inside are more centered and authentic and are inspired by their lives; they're not affected by manic fantasies and their cohort depressions. They're clear, they're objective; they use reason, and they use the advanced part of their brains to govern their amygdala base survival impulses and instincts which polarize or imbalance their neurochemistry.

The amygdala deals with impulses and instincts, the remaining portion of the limbic brain deals with intermediate emotions, and the highest part of the brain deals with objective reason and intuition. When that area of the brain is active, we don't generally have depression. It's in the amygdala-based responses that we have runaway mania and depression, because we're striving for a fantasy of one-sidedness and trying to avoid the nightmare that comes with it.

The Buddha said the desire for that which is unavailable and the desire to avoid that which is unavoidable are the source of human suffering. If you're striving for something that is one-sided but unavailable and trying to get rid of the other side, which is unavoidable, you're probably going to "suffer" from depression. But the depression is not your enemy. It is also your friend because it is letting you know that you are pursuing unrealistic expectations and giving you feedback in order to adjust your course. It is there to help you to set realistic objectives, in realistic times with realistic strategies and be authentic. Imagine this whole emotional swinging scenario as a magnet, with both positive and negative poles. Can you get a magnet that has one end without the other? No, but if you're striving for it, you're going to have frustration and futility, and you're going to be angry because you can't get it.

Much of depression is the result of comparisons of your current reality to these fantasies. That affects your brain chemistry. When you're functioning from within your higher brain center, you balance your chemistry. When you function from down into your lower brain center, you imbalance your chemistry, because you're polarized, and that's a very important component of depression.

Someone who is suicidally depressed is saying, "I can't live like this any longer." I've gotten many of those cases. I help them go within and look at the contents of their mind, because you can't have a feeling in your physiology without content in your mind. You may not be cognizant of it because you haven't asked the optimal questions, but you will not have a polarized feeling without an imbalanced perception and subjectively distorted expectation and thought content behind it.

Memory and Anti-Memory

When you're depressed, what exactly is in your mind? What are you comparing it to? If you write out everything that's in your mind under "depression" and then find its exact opposite, you'll discover that your mind has both a memory and an anti-memory. It has the polar opposite in the mind at the same time. If one is depressing, the other is elating: this anti-content is the reciprocal opposite.

If you're infatuated with somebody, you assume that individual has more positives than negatives. The week after the first date, you can't get them out of your mind. Your imbalanced perception of them is creating brain noise in you. If all of a sudden, they say, "I'm sorry; I won't date you anymore; don't call me again," you'll be depressed, because you're comparing your current reality to a fantasy about what this new relationship was going to lead to. You wouldn't, and couldn't, have that depression without a previous or current elation or fantasy.

Then imagine you're in a relationship in which you're angry and bitter. You're tired and worn out, and you're saying, "This is enough." The other individual finally calls you and says, "I'm leaving the relationship." You're not depressed; you go out and celebrate with your friends.

You experience grief and depression over the loss of what you're infatuated with, but you experience relief and elation over the loss of what you've resented. That means you couldn't have depression unless you had some sort of an addiction to a fantasy about how it was expected and going to be.

That's a key source of your depression. You may not be paying attention to it, because you've been told by society and everybody else to be "happy." "Don't be sad. Be kind; don't be cruel; be positive, don't be negative." They're promoting the opium of the masses by feeding you an idea that you can be one-sided, a moral hypocrisy, but the truth is, you're not going to be one-sided. No one is. It's insane to try to expect a one-sided life when the truth is, you have both. You don't need to get rid of any part of yourself in order to love and appreciate yourself. Beware of outer projected moral hypocrisies.

As long as you unrealistically expect others or yourself to be one-sided, you're going to be depressed. You're also going to be depressed if you're expecting others in the world to always live in your set of values and not their own.

The ABCDEFGHIs of Negativity

I'd like to go over some of the most common behaviors I've found in clinically depressed people. I don't know of anyone who is clinically depressed that has come to my seminars without one or more of these behaviors. They are the by-product of delusions—unrealistic expectations and fantasies that lead to the ABCDEFGHIs of negativity:

- Anger
- Aggression
- Blame
- Betrayal (feelings of)
- Criticism
- Challenge
- Despair
- Despondent
- Exit and Escape (a desire to)
- Frustration
- Hatred

- Grouchiness
- Grief
- Hatred
- Feeling Hurt
- Irritability
- Irrationality

Because human beings have each of these emotional feelings, you're not going to eliminate them. They are not your enemy; they're your friends.

Depression is not an illness in my perspective. Depression's not your enemy. It's feedback to let you know that you have unrealistic expectations. Psychologists and psychiatrists object to that idea because it challenges their current model of false attribution-based reality and their profession's mechanism of making an income, since you can do this on your own. No organization will annihilate its reasons for existence.

The Causes of Depression

Here are some of the more common causes of depression:

1. An unrealistic expectation of another individual to live in a one-sided manner. Imagine you're in a relationship with somebody, and you're expecting them to be always up, never down; always positive, never negative; always supportive, never challenging. Can they be? No, but if you have that expectation—even a little more than 50/50—it's unrealistic, because they are going to express both sides. Besides, as we've heard, a balance of

support and challenge enables you to maximally grow and be resilient and fit.

2. An unrealistic expectation of others to live inside your values and outside their own. As we've seen, people make decisions based on what they believe will give them the greatest advantage over disadvantage in respect to their own highest values. So, if you expect them to live in your values and not theirs, the ABCDs . . . of negativity are going to surface. Almost every marriage has this: "You're supposed to live by my values. You should be doing this." Whenever you hear somebody say, "You should," "You ought," "You're supposed to," "You've got to," "You have to," or "You must," they're self-righteously projecting their values onto you and expecting you to live by them. If you're saying the same things, you're self-righteously projecting your higher values onto them, and expecting them to read your mind and do what you think is important.

No wonder you're depressed. You have an unrealistic expectation. They can't consistently live up to your values. The only time they can appear to be doing so is when they're initially and temporarily infatuated with you, blind and willing to sacrifice for a short time. But you'll pay a price, because whenever they sacrifice for you, they'll retain it in their memory, and eventually you'll pay. For they will store their sacrifices in their memory and eventually retaliate with their unrealistic expectations. That's not how they're going to live. They're going to live according to their own hierarchy of values, not yours.

3. The third is a combination of the first two. You expect this individual to be one-sided *and* to live in your higher values. I've seen people in my seminars where the wife or the husband says, "You're supposed to know what I want. You're supposed to know what is on my mind by now, and I'll punish you until you figure it out." In other words, instead of just speaking up and saying, "This is my expectation" and seeing if it's realistic and respectful, I'm just going to punish you in the meantime.

   I've seen this. It doesn't generally lead to some of the most immediately fulfilling outcomes, of course. It's a recipe for a more than challenging relationship dynamic, but it is also a feedback mechanism. If you expect your partner to live in your values, you're going to experience frustration and futility. They're not going to; they're going to live according to their own set of values. If you expect them to be one-sided, it's unrealistic too, but it's commonly why people are depressed. If you put those two sets of expectations together, you've got a double whammy.

4. The fourth one is an unrealistic expectation on oneself to live in a one-sided manner. I call this the "always" positive mental attitude delusion. It's imagining that you are or should be thinking positive most all the time. If you do, you'll find out that you're lying to yourself and have become a hypocrite.

   You can't live striving to be one-sided. If you do, you'll end up angry at yourself. You'll feel proud when you're positive and ashamed when you aren't. You'll end up a bit bipolar, because the addiction to one-sided outcomes will split you apart. Be honest with yourself: do an inventory. You'll find that you oscillate. But your mind has a psychological set point striving to maintain homeostasis.

By the way, I've met many self-help teachers or gurus that promote positive thinking; I know many of them individually. They're not always positive; they're both positive and negative, just like you and me and everybody else. If you're comparing yourself to your one-sided assumption about them instead of honoring who you are, you're more likely to become depressed, because you're going to live in the fantasy that they really are that way: they've figured it out, and you haven't. But the reality is, they're just human beings with both sides—like you and me.

5. An unrealistic expectation of yourself to live outside your own values and inside those of other people. As we've seen, when you're infatuated with somebody, you'll temporarily sacrifice what's important to you to be with them. Within days or weeks, that will fade. You'll want your own life back, and your life is based on your own set of values, because your identity and primary mission revolves around your highest values.

You're not going to be able to live in other people's values. As I've mentioned, many people have a fantasy of obtaining financial independence, but they don't have the hierarchy of values that will lead them to achieve it. If you don't have a high value on serving, creating sustainable fair exchange, saving, investing and accumulating more interest-bearing assets than liabilities, you're not likely to become financially independent; you're going to keep spending your money on depreciating consumable items that are higher on your list of values, and keep remaining financially burdened or in debt. But if you still have unrealistic expectations about building financial wealth, you're very likely to become depressed. Your hierarchy of values is making your decisions for you, and if you try to live outside them, you're likely to have one or more of the ABCDs . . . of negativity.

6. The sixth one is a combination of four and five. Here you're expecting yourself both to be one-sided and to live in someone else's values that you admire. Emerson warned against it: "Envy is ignorance. Imitation is suicide." Trying to be somebody you're not is not going to work, because the magnificence of who you truly are is far greater than the fantasies you impose on yourself. When you live by your highest values, you have more realistic expectations, and fulfillment. When you try to live up to other people's expectations, it's like trying to be Elvis. You'll be second at being somebody else. Why not be first at being you?

7. Number seven is a combination of the first three and the second three. Now you have a double whammy. You have an expectation for both you and others to be imbalanced and one-sided, and you expect everybody to live in somebody else's values. Now you're angry at others and yourself because they and you are not matching your unrealistic expectations of reality. Again, you're creating a fantasy that people in the world can't satisfy.

8. Next comes an unrealistic expectation of the people in the world in general and/or—some anthropomorphic local or universal God—to live one-sidedly. I've seen people pray to an anthropomorphic God made in their own image and value system, to protect them from their own anxieties. They pray, "Dear God, give me everything I want. Protect me from anything I don't want." Now this is partly a dissociated delusion, but billions of people do it. They expect the world to be one-sided and to match what they want: peace without war, positive without negative, support without challenge, protection without aggression. When something challenges their values, they're angry, and they disassociate from it. They create a fantasy about how life is supposed to be, and they become addicted to that utopic fantasy. Of course, there are many sales specialists ready to sell them the opium and fantasy they seek.

9. An unrealistic expectation of the people in the world in general and/or—some anthropomorphic local or universal God—to live inside your values. Imagine getting up in the morning and saying, "Dear world, universe, or God, I want the whole world to match everything I fantasize and want. Please take care of that." That's a bit delusional. Of course, everybody else is doing the same, all with a different set of values, so either you have a crazy God that's in chaos trying to figure that out or you have a delusion that there's some form of an anthropomorphic God that's actually going to do it.

The more reasonable and grounded probability is that you are going to live according to your hierarchy of values, and everyone else is going to live according to theirs. Each organism is trying to fulfill their more basic survival mechanisms, and the world is based on living organisms that are trying to survive and thrive. If you have unrealistic expectations, there's no way you can get those met; you're going to end up being angry and aggressive and blame the world. This non-resilient state of mind will probably leave you a bit depressed to say the least.

I once worked with a lady in Dallas whose son was a motocross guy who did flips and stunts professionally. She used to pray, "Dear God, protect him from getting injured." She was anxious and frightened, and she prayed every single day. Every day her son didn't get injured, she was thinking, "God is protecting him." Then one day he got into a major accident and practically became a quadriplegic.

Now this woman was angry at the same God she had created in her own mind: he didn't protect her. She was depressed and angry and bitter, blaming God. She didn't want to go to church, because God had let her down. She had an unrealistic expectation because she had been praying to an imagined anthropomorphic fantasy image that she'd created in her mind, and she was depressed.

Her son then went to a chiropractor, got adjusted, and started bringing back his nervous functions and eventually fully recovered. When he became inspired by the amazing results of his chiropractor care, he decided to become a chiropractor, earned his doctorate degree and opened up a clinic and built a viable practice. He then began sponsoring motocross events. His mother started to say, "Oh, maybe God did something right after all."

Similarly, people sometimes have unrealistic expectations of the world or society in general, including politicians and people in power, or even of their anthropomorphic god.

10. This is a combination of eight and nine. You have an unrealistic expectation on a bigger scale, on people in society as a whole, on the world in general or on some anthropomorphic God, and you're also expecting all of these to live by your values.

11. Number eleven is a combination of three and six and ten. Now you're really going for full-blown, major depression. You're probably a suicide case by now, because you live in complete delusion about how life is "supposed" to be, or going to be.

12. Unrealistic expectations of mechanical objects to function one-sidedly. You've probably been angry at your computer or your garage-door opener. If you expect any mechanical object to do anything other than what it was designed to do, you're going to be upset. If you don't put gas in your car and it stops on the road, you get angry at it: "I can't believe this car did that to me!" You have an unrealistic expectation that the mechanical object will do something other than what it is mechanically designed to do.

13. You could also have an unrealistic expectation for mechanical objects to live inside your values. I've

known people who, even though they know they're overspending, go online and get mad at the computer for not giving them a positive cash flow. They're not looking at themselves and their actions; they're blaming the computer or the bank. Whenever you are unrealistic and imbalanced in your expectations, you're going to be angry, aggressive, and blame. You feel betrayed, criticized, challenged, despairing, and depressed. You want to exit and escape the situation, feel frustrated and futile, and you're going to be grouchy and grieving. But you've set it up yourself.

Clinical depression is a comparison of your current reality which is balanced, to an unrealistic expectation, a fantasy, which is imbalanced. You're assuming that if all of these unrealistic expectations actually occurred, you'd be happy. The addiction to that fantasy is leading to your depression.

People in my seminars who are clinically depressed have been told by their psychiatrists that they need medication because they have a biochemical imbalance. They come up to me, and I say, "So you're clinically depressed, huh?"

"Yeah, for the last two years. I haven't been able to function. I've stopped working."

I make sure that they don't have disability insurance or the military economically covering that problem. Because if they're getting more money out of disability than they were earning at work, quite possibly they won't want to go back to a job that provides less. Otherwise, I sit down and ask questions, to calm down their unrealistic expectations of how others, themselves, or the world is supposed to be and to appreciate their current reality as it is, which will sometimes dissolve their depression in the seminar quite efficiently.

Famous for Depression

Let me explain how to dissolve these fantasies. At one point I was at the Swiss Hotel in Sydney talking to a lady who said, "I have a friend that was for a time quite clinically depressed but has now become quite famous for his depression. He published a book and interviewed some celebrities that were also experiencing depression. He's known now for being on a cause to help people with depression.

"He almost committed suicide, and he ended up on medication. Slowly but surely, he came back, and he's functioning. I'd like to have you talk with him."

I met with him at the hotel. After a brief introduction and some rapport building questions, I asked, "You're now a leader in the field of depression. Do you think it's to your advantage to know every possible tool that could help people with depression?"

"Yes."

"If I were to tell you about a possible alternative, a new way of dealing with depression, would you by chance love to know about it?"

"If there was something out there, I would know about it. I've been studying the field, and I'm current with it; there's nothing out there that I haven't seen."

"What if there was? Would you be willing to hear about it?"

"What is it?"

"It's a series of questions to ask yourself."

"Yeah, I know: cognitive stuff. None of that works. The only thing that has worked is medication."

"What if there was something that would empower people without depending on a drug? Would you be at least receptive to hearing about it?"

He was being partly sponsored by the pharmaceutical industry, so I was going against his grain here. He was a little resistant.

I thought, "I'm going to go in for the jugular." I said, "Do you mind if I do a demonstration here on your own individual life?"

"How?"

"Would you do me a favor and just go to the moment when you were depressed and suicidal and you wanted to take your life? Just go to that moment in your mind."

"I'd rather not."

"Please, I just want to share with you some insightful questions. I promise it'll be worth it."

"OK."

He went back to the moment when he was thinking about taking his life and really feeling it.

At that moment, I said, "Depression is a comparison of your current reality to a fantasy—an unrealistic expectation that's not happening. If you have a fantasy, your life becomes a nightmare, because you're striving for a one-sided pole, and the other pole smacks you. So let's go to that moment.

"Are you there? In that moment, when you're going to take your life, you're comparing your life to what you wish it would be. It's not happening. What is the expectation that you had at that moment that was unmet?"

"I know what it is," he said. "I had a job at a company, I was climbing up the corporate ladder, and I was just about to get where I wanted to go position-wise, because the guy in that position was leaving. I just knew I was the one for that job, but the company took somebody from the outside and stuck him in there. It pissed me off royally. I did what I could to try to undermine this guy, and we started to clash. He fired me, although I didn't think I could be fired.

"All of a sudden I was out, and I was enraged and bitter. I was angry and aggressive. I blamed and felt betrayed. I criticized; I challenged. I felt despaired and depressed. I had hatred and hurt in my mind. As a result, I went into depression and wanted to take my life, because my ideal—fantasy—position and world was taken from me."

"Let's go back to that moment," I said. "If you had gotten the position you were expecting, what would the drawbacks have been?"

"There would have been no drawbacks."

"By my definition, a one-sided, all positive outcome is a fantasy. As long as you see no drawbacks in your fantasy world, about how it should have been, would have been, could have been, you won't appreciate your life by comparison. That's not real; what's real is what happened. So what would the drawbacks have been?"

I made him go through and identify drawback after drawback—ones he was certain about, not speculations. I asked, "If you'd had gotten that job, what income would you have had?" He told me. "Twenty years later, where would it be?" He told me that too. "Right now, you're a best-selling author, hanging out with celebrities, and getting endorsement funding. Where are you now?" He told me three times that amount.

"Would you have gotten celebrity status?"

"No."

"Would you have ever written a book?"

"No."

"Would you ever get to meet all the people you've met?"

"No."

"Would you have the platform to do what you do today?"

"No."

"Where would you be?"

"Working for somebody else, stuck in a frigging job with a more fixed income."

All of a sudden, he started to see the downsides to his fantasy that up until that moment he never questioned or confronted. I didn't stop until the upsides equaled the downsides on his current life and the fantasy was broken. I leveled the playing field to the point where there was nothing left except thank you for the event and for his current life.

"Now try to find your depression," I went on. "I dare you to find it. Just try to access it with your mind."

He couldn't. He said, "Right now I can't get to it."

"The only reason you could get to it before is that you were holding on to an unrealistic expectation and fantasy. The brain/mind attempts to maintain homeostasis upon being polarized, and so you won't have a fantasy without an accompanying nightmare. You don't have elation without depression, a philia without a phobia, or any magnet that has one side or pole only. People who embrace both poles simultaneously are the ones who go out and do something extra with resilience, and the people striving for one side get smacked by the other side."

That's the hard knocks. The fantasy is soft and easy— immediate gratification. "I want support without challenge. I want kindness without receiving the cruel.

"You don't have a drug deficiency; you don't have a biochemical imbalance cause, although you may have a correlation," I went on. "It got imbalanced because in your subconscious mind, you stored a split unconscious fantasy and conscious nightmare. That creates noise in the brain, which takes you out of your executive center. It shuts you down, and you go down into the amygdala. Now you're striving for that which is unavailable and trying to avoid that which is unavoidable.

"You've been taking medication, thinking you have an imbalance, but the imbalance is a feedback mechanism letting you know that you had gotten off your highest valued sourced mission. Right now, you are on your mission and didn't even recognize it."

"You're quite convincing," he said.

This man's crisis was his blessing, because he had been trapped in a job for security instead of doing a more purposeful pursuit that was inspiring and meaningful, as he was now. The one who took away his job, whom he thought was evil, was an angel in disguise.

"Now I've initiated within you a potential challenge or problem," I continued, "because you're promoting a biochemical imbalance and pharmaceutical model, which in many, if not most, cases may just not be the actual cause, correlation maybe, but cause no, and you're possibly going to distract people from reclaiming their power. You may never want to see me again, but I was suggested by a friend to meet with you to say all of this to you because you have influence, and you could possibly bring both messages out."

Depressed in South Africa

Once I had a lady attend my Breakthrough Experience seminar in South Africa. She was from Eastern Europe, and she had married a man and come to South Africa. She claimed that she was severely depressed and on medication for her biochemical imbalance. I said, "When you're depressed, you're comparing your current reality to some expectation that's unrealistic and certainly not real right now. So what are you comparing your currently unfulfilled life to?"

"I moved to another country," the woman said. "I had a man who promised me a lot of benefits and lifestyle upgrades if I moved, but he didn't live up to it. He didn't do what he said he was going to do. I had a kid with him, and then he left me. Now I'm trapped. I have no money and I have no job, and I've not been able to do what I really want to do, which is art and painting."

"What are you comparing your present perceived predicament of life to?"

"I would have been happy if I'd just stayed home and never met the man."

"So if you'd stayed home in that country and never met this man or had experienced this more ideal scenario, what would be some of the drawbacks?"

"There wouldn't be any drawbacks. I'd be happy."

"There are generally two sides to events in life—the benefit side and drawback side. What would be some of the drawbacks of doing that?" I had to push and shake her a bit to get to the real and more objective truth.

"I'd be in an area of the world that was even lower socioeconomically. I'd probably be trapped in that country. I'd probably never have had the opportunities I had when I came to South Africa. I wouldn't have my child." When she said that, she started bawling.

Now she might have had another child, but we have no proof that that would have been a greater or more fulfilling deal. We can hold fantasies about how life should have been and could have been and would have been, but again, the reality is what's happening. If you can't see how your current reality is a benefit and quit comparing it to fantasies about how it could have been, you're not going to appreciate your life as it actually and currently is.

I made the woman face the drawbacks about what would have happened if she'd stayed in her native country, and the benefits of coming to South Africa. It helped her become independent. If she'd had a man who had taken care of her there, she might not have had her additional education or artistic career.

I helped identify the drawbacks of her fantasy and the benefits of her current reality until she had tears of gratitude in her eyes. She gave me a big hug and said, "I'm not feeling depressed right now."

"No, because your depression was due to your comparison of your current reality to a fantasy you were holding on to about yourself or other people and your home country."

Although people may have been told they have a biochemical imbalance, they could be storing subconscious delusions, unrealistic expectations, angers, and polarities that are throwing their chemistry off. If you work through them methodically, step by step, you can do amazing transformations and help people grow past their so-called depression.

Again, there may be real cases of biochemical imbalance, but they're much rarer than we're told. Many more people are on medication than is essential or optimal. I've seen many people come off medication and never go back to it once they learned how to clear their fantasies and unrealistic expectations and begin to appreciate their present.

Moreover, if you undergo this process, you empower your life. You become a master of destiny, not a victim of history. You empower yourself by living congruently with your highest values instead of living in fantasy and trying to get immediate gratification from your amygdala's impulses. Get real, get empowered, and get balanced, and watch what happens to your physiology and psychology and watch how more resilient you become.

If you've been depressed, you don't have to stay that way. There are perceptions, decisions, and actions you can do on your own to empower your life. I've tried to give you some insights about how.

Again, the quality of your life is based on the quality of the questions you ask yourself. If you ask questions that bring balance to your mind, you liberate yourself from fantasies and emotional polarities so you can appreciate your realities. The magnificence of who you are is far greater than any fantasies you'll ever impose on yourself.

Chapter 7

Coping with Anxiety

You may have faced a situation in your life where you felt anxious, phobic, or concerned about the future, so I'd like to discuss what anxiety is and what you can do to resolve it. I've been working with this issue for many years, and what I will share may appear to be quite novel. You probably won't find this information anywhere else.

Blue Jeans, White Shirt

Say you're a child and you see and hear your mother and father fighting. Your father gets aggressive and starts hitting your mom and she yells back. You don't want to see or hear that. You run off to your room, hide under the bed, close your eyes, and cover up your ears. You try to fall asleep that way to avoid the experience.

The next morning, you get up and the fight's over, but you're still having a subconsciously stored experience of this—assumed to be only—painful event that you saw the night before.

Let's say you go grocery shopping with your mom the next day. You see a man in the aisle who is wearing blue jeans and a white shirt, which is what your father was wearing during the fight. Those same color clothes items trigger an association that makes you remember that event. You're not really paying attention to the man who's walking by, but you pick up the associated colorful clothes cues, which are saying, "There's something about this man that I don't feel comfortable about." You've made associations in your brain because of the similarity of this man's blue jeans and white shirt.

Say your father has brown hair. A day later, you might see some man walk by with blue jeans, a white shirt, but blond, not brown, hair. Now you're making a secondary association between blond hair and blue jeans and a white shirt. Now when you see somebody with blue jeans, a white shirt, and blond hair, you don't feel comfortable with him.

Associations can be visual or auditory or from any other primary sensory stimuli modality. You probably remember moments where somebody's voice reminded you of someone you didn't trust because that individual lied to you or didn't do what they said they'd do. As a result, that voice can trigger an anxious, withdrawing feeling in you. Associations can also have to do with smells or tastes. Someone is wearing a perfume that reminds you of somebody you broke up with twenty years ago, and consequently, you don't like that individual.

Layers upon layers of associations can build up. Associations can be primary, secondary, or tertiary. Anxiety is a secondary or tertiary association complex in the brain whereby a collection of stimuli is triggering unconscious responses to an initial event that was perceived to be painful or fearful. Almost anything that is extremely painful could initiate secondary associations, creating anxiety.

I've known people who were drinking alcohol and had a great time. Then all of a sudden, the police raided and threw them in jail. The next time they look at a bottle of alcohol, they immediately think of that event: "I can't touch alcohol after that. I just don't want to touch it. It just makes me sick to my stomach," because they almost puked when they went to jail.

You could also have pleasurable associations. Someone may come into your life that reminds you of a former lover who may have been unbelievably kind to you but moved out of town. Now you're hooked by someone who has the same appearance or smell.

Imbalances of Perception

Like many of the issues we've already explored, anxieties are due to nothing more than imbalances of perception and their later compounded associations. A phobia is an assumption that there's about to be more pains than pleasures, more negatives than positives, more losses than gains. A philia is an assumption that there's about to be more pleasures than pains, more positives than negatives, more gains than losses. Both phobias and philias can trigger secondary and tertiary association responses. You've got a positive fantasy or a negative anxiety disorder. The positive fantasy disorder is sometimes called a *hook*, which gets us to repeat the same impulsive behaviors.

Emotional mood disorders are a result of missing information. You are missing or unconscious or ignorant of the downsides in the philia or fantasy, and you are missing or unconscious or ignorant of the upsides in the phobia or anxiety. The disorder actually has a hidden order underlying it once you discover the missing information. Experiencing the disorder offers you an opportunity to become aware of what you have not yet intuitively become consciously aware of. Once aware of it, you get to rebalance your mind and bring back the awareness of the ever-present love that surrounds and permeates your life. It is offering you feedback to help you become more empowered, authentic, and resilient.

Addictions can be caused by perceptions of pleasure with their secondary or tertiary associations. People do it with food; they do it with relationships. They have the same patterns and cycles as with anxiety and phobias. But we don't typically run away from those things and call them bad, because the addictions are pleasures or advantages that we keep seeking. We seek help for anxieties, but positive hooks are just as disruptive to our lives or at any rate as challenging to the body.

What do we do about these survival-based, impulse or instinct generating, positive or negative associations? To begin with, for each association you've made, your brain sets up an anti-association. In other words, when you've had a traumatic or painful experience that you think has "caused" you pain without a pleasure, you will dissociate from that. Using iconography from your previous experiences, your brain/mind will create a fantasy image of pleasure without pain to compensate, and for the purpose of physiological and psychological homeostasis.

Again, nightmares rarely occur without accompanying fantasies. The mind balances pairs of opposites. But we typically become conscious of one and unconscious of the other. If we're conscious of the negatives, along with secondary and tertiary associations, and we're unconscious of the positives, we can create an anxiety disorder. I designed questions that are found within the Demartini Method that help individuals become aware or conscious of what they are unconscious of to balance their mental equation.

Pleasure alongside Pain

But say I can show you exactly the moment where the pleasure was alongside the pain, where the gain was alongside. Then I can dissolve that anxiety; it's quite amazing how fast this can be done. When you experience anxiety, the associations in your brain have simply been stacked up so that the other side of the equation, the other end of the magnet, has not been revealed to you.

With anxiety, you're conscious of the negatives and unconscious of the positives. If the primary event or the secondary or tertiary associations are not brought simultaneously into balance, they can be stored in the subconscious mind and keep running progressively expanding loops, making you still more anxious. I've seen people get anxious to the point where many subtle seemingly innocuous stimuli are triggering their anxiety, and they're living with this fear all the time.

It doesn't have to be that way. What I do is very simple. I direct the subject to go to that moment where and when they perceived themselves experiencing an event that they regarded as painful, repulsive, or traumatic. Take anything that you associate in the brain with a repulsive response, itemize it, and go into the episodic moment. You may say, "I don't want to go back and recall that." But it's very valuable to do it, because if you go back and get present in that moment, your intuition has access to the other counterbalancing side, which liberates you from the imbalanced memory.

Neuron magazine had a beautiful article talking about memories and anti-memories. It said that the brain, when it has a memory, will inhibit or facilitate certain neural pathways and their resultant functions. At the same time, it will create an anti-memory that will facilitate or inhibit other functions to balance the memory in order to keep the brain's chemistry and electricity balanced and save it from brain noise, static, or chaos. When people are not balanced, they may end up with schizoid behavior, bipolar conditions, and other neurological concerns.

By becoming present and looking at the exact moment where and when you perceived yourself or somebody else demonstrating the specific trait and action that you dislike or avoid, you itemize the episodic content. What exactly is there? What are you actually seeing? What are you hearing? What are you smelling? What are you tasting? What are you feeling? Get as much detail as possible—the content, the context, the where, the when, the what, the why—in as much detail as possible. What exactly is occurring, and who are they doing this to? Is it you or somebody else? Self or other? Once we have that data, you can then allow your intuition to reveal its complementary opposite or flip side and find the exact anti-memory data. You'll find out that your brain will have experienced exactly the opposite at the same time, but you were unaware of it.

When I do this for other individuals, it's mind-blowing. People say, "I had no idea that information was there." The mind maintains a complete pair of opposites, but we split it up into conscious and unconscious parts.

As we've seen, so-called mental "dysfunctions" are the result of an imbalance—perceiving the benefits without the drawbacks, or vice versa. Either way, it takes some time for most people to get past the imbalance and discover the other side. But you can have the wisdom of the ages (without the aging process) by seeing both sides simultaneously, which you can do if you ask the optimal questions as I designed in the Demartini Method. In fact, your intuition is trying to point the other side out to you. If you look carefully and get present with the moment, your intuition will pop it up.

Using the Demartini Method to deal with these anxieties and fears, I've found out that both sides are simultaneously accessible within three seconds of getting present in the moment. But it's advisable to get down into an episodic moment—the details of content, context, where, when, and so on, in order to awaken it.

The Moment of Trauma

The mind will tend to dissociate from anything that's perceived to be a torture or traumatic and will create a simultaneous ecstasy association to balance it. I've had people who have been beaten and broken: they initiated a freeze response and dissociated and created compensatory fantasies in order to survive, but they didn't realize they were doing that until I took them back to the moment of the perceived trauma, when their mind dissociated and created a fantasy in order to survive and maintain homeostasis in the brain/mind. This happens in beatings, rapes, and auto accidents. When you have a pain without a pleasure, the mind will automatically create a dissociated opposite: a pleasure without a pain to equilibrate the mind.

In one case, I brought a lady back to the moment when she was trying to commit suicide. She was thinking life wasn't matching how she wanted and fantasized it to be, so she wanted to end it. She was overdosing on heroin, and her mind dissociated and created the complete opposite fantasy of her perceived so-called traumatic life. She felt responsible for her parents' divorce. She didn't know how to handle the idea (even though it wasn't factual) that she was responsible for her parents splitting. As a teenager, she started drinking and doing heroin to escape her sense of responsibility for the split—the subdiction.

When I had her go back into that moment of her attempted suicide, her mind was dissociated, and she was holding her mother and father in her mind in her fantasy world. They were walking through a field with butterflies and birds, and she was envisioning a fantasy life, with her parents joined together, and she was holding their hands and keeping them together. She had a complete anti-memory going on to balance out her memory. She felt she was causing the parental split in her sorrowful memory, but in her fantasy world, her anti-memory, she was joining them together and putting them into a state of joy.

Sorrow, joy. Pain, pleasure. The mind has both of them simultaneously as memory and anti-memory. If you perceive the downsides without the upsides and you associate anything with it, you can have a phobia or have anxiety responses. If you perceive the upside without perceiving the downside, you can have philic, fantasy responses, such as addictive behaviors. If you can see both of them at the same time, the whole dynamic pops and you become present and feel gratitude and love.

When I showed this woman the exact moment when she was in this torture, she saw where her fantasy was and put them together. She was brought to tears and realized that her mind wasn't tortured; it actually is a simultaneous balancing act. I define love as a balance of opposites synchronously put back together. All of a sudden, she felt loved; she felt whole again.

When I am working with somebody who has an anxiety, I go into the actual moment of the initial event perceived to be provoking pain and fear. I can show them where the other side is and pop the original so-called torture trauma or whatever else has initiated the fear. Once it's neutralized and I show them both sides, they don't have a memory of a pain without a pleasure, or a pleasure without a pain. They see the balance. They feel appreciated and loved in that moment. They realize there's nothing to fix. They discover a hidden order within their apparent disorder. They discovered and became mindfully present with the once missing information.

Many times, if I am able or permitted to access the original event, and neutralize it, the cascading secondary ones simply dissolve. If I get only a secondary or a tertiary association, or some later trigger, I can peel it back like an onion and go back to the original one. Either way, I eventually get there. Sometimes if I'm dealing with a secondary or tertiary association, I may go to that one and clear it. Then I go to the next memory, find the anti-memory, and clear it. I can do this layer by layer, eventually getting back to the original event, if there's a recall of that, or I can just go back to the original one.

Let's say you've been in a house where a fire has broken out. You've got smoke in the house, and you're freaking out: the door's locked, you can't get out, and you're having anxiety and fear. I can take you through each moment in your mind frame by frame. If I put each of your memories and anti-memories together, second by second, frame by frame, all the way back until you've gone through that entire experience, I guarantee you, you won't, and can't, experience anxiety.

When I do this with people, they're blown away. Sometimes they've been treated for anxiety disorders for months or years, but nobody ever brought the pairs of opposites together in the brain at the same time. The moment you do, it all dissolves. It's over with.

The process may feel difficult if you've never done it, but I assure you it's methodical, it's sequential, and it works. As long as we are repressing the unconscious, a tool like this one can help us bring the counterbalancing unconscious perceptions simultaneously to the conscious level to awaken full consciousness, sometimes termed mindfulness.

Get All the Details

Let's go through it again. Go to the moment where and when you perceived yourself or others displaying or demonstrating a specific trait, action, or inaction that you despise, dislike, hate, resent, or avoid, that you found negative or painful. Go to that moment. Are you there? Where are you? When are you? What exactly is happening? What's the context? What's driving it? What is the sight? What is the sound? What is the feel? What is the smell? What is the taste? Get as many modalities as you can. Get as much detail as you can. Write it out.

Once you get it down, take the opposite. If it's a dark room, where is there light? If it's loud, where's the softer noise? If it's fast moving, where is it slow? The anti-memory will be there to balance out the memory. The second those two are brought to your awareness at the same time, you'll have full consciousness. Your intuition is constantly attempting to reveal this balance to you. And full consciousness, I assure you, does not have anxiety. It unveils and reveals a spatial and temporal entanglement of content and anti-content in the mind synchronously.

I did this recently with a young lady who was having anxiety disorder because of a perceptually "traumatic" event that occurred while she was out partying with her friends on a street corner. This tragic event led to her being taken to the hospital. She ended up having heart palpitations. She started having anxiety, and she was placed and somewhat dependent on medication. She was having emotional anxiety outbursts, and she didn't want to go out and interact with people because she was having secondary cascading associations triggering fear.

The mother brought her to me, and I went methodically through each slivered moment of the initial "traumatic" episode that she stated initiated the anxiety reaction, one by one. We took each momentary sliver of time, did the Demartini Method, found the other side, and brought full consciousness to her awareness. Then I said, "Now that you see both of these sides together, what's your representation in the brain?"

"I don't have any anxiety. It doesn't frighten me."

"No, because you see both sides. Now see if you can initiate your response to anxiety. See if you can think of anything that might trigger it."

She just smiled at me and said, "I can't do it."

"No, you can't, because your brain does not have a one-sided perception anymore, which initiated the anxious or phobic instinct to avoid. Both sides have been brought to your awareness, so it's over with."

It's hard to believe that most people haven't been taught this; many don't even believe that there is another, unconscious part of the mind that contains the other side of the experience. But once you do, it's eye-opening. In actuality, both sides are going on, but we keep dividing our experiences up with conscious-unconscious splits. We subjectively bias our perception and filter out half of what's there. As a result, we have an emotion that is distracting us instead of realizing that there's a balancing act of love going on every moment of our lives.

If I put the positive and negative associated and dissociated content together, they both dissolve, and there's just a centered, calm, poised, present, neutral state. It's very empowering when you realize that. Once you learn how to do this, you realize that no matter what goes on in your life, you have the power to awaken the unconscious, bring it to consciousness, and have nothing but appreciation and centeredness. This maximizes your resilience since there is no fear of loss of the philic positive pole and no fear of gain of the phobic negative pole remaining.

Once you master that skill, nothing on the outside necessarily has to have an impact on your life. You can neutralize any of those perceptions and distractions. If you ask questions that allow you to see both sides, making you fully conscious of the unconscious and conscious together, nothing can distract you, and anxiety is a thing of the past. You don't have to live with anxiety.

You can't have fear unless you perceive and anticipate more negatives than positives. You can't have a fantasy unless you perceive you are about to experience more positives than negatives. Once you perceive both sides at the same time, nothing is inherently either good or bad, philic or phobic, until we subjectively mislabel it so. It's a combination of the two at once, like a magnet. If you want magnetism, drawing to you what you want in life, you want to be able to see both ends of the magnet at once.

Many of the psychological disorders, like anxiety and depression, are feedback mechanisms to tell us what we've lied to ourselves about our reality. And this feedback is making sure we leave no event unloved. Anything you can't say thank you for in your life is baggage. Anything you can say thank you for is fuel. Reclaim your center, allow your intuition to awaken your authentic self, and maximize your resilience and fitness.

Chapter 8

Moving Past Grief

Around 1976, I went on a surfing trip to El Salvador. I would surf from early in the morning and come in for something to eat at about eleven o'clock.

One day after I had my breakfast-lunch, I walked through the town in La Libertad, which is outside of San Salvador, toward and on the beach. I saw a procession of about 200 people walking through the streets. They'd closed off the main street, and the people were dressed in whites and colors. There was celebration and music. It looked like a parade. I wanted to know what it was, and I walked up and tried to find somebody who could speak some English. Finally, I came across a young man, and I said, "What's happening? What's the celebration about?"

"Our mayor has died."

I was somewhat shocked. I wasn't expecting that, because it looked like a celebration more than a mourning of a death.

I followed the procession down to the cemetery. They put the casket into the ground. People danced, celebrated, and had a feast.

The young man said that they were celebrating the freedom of this man's spirit. "He's free. He's not bonded to the body anymore."

I thought, "That's an interesting perspective." It threw off my ideas of grief and death. Until that point, I assumed that death was something that you're solemn about. You don't speak. You may be depressed, and people are grieving and crying.

At that moment I thought, "That's interesting, the same initial stimulus, a death of somebody could lead to either mourning or celebration."

For the time being, I just stored that information. I wasn't interested in clinical applications yet. A few years later, I noticed that in some countries, when people attended a funeral, they were dressed in black, covering their faces, and it was solemn and quiet. It was the complete polar opposite to what I'd seen in El Salvador. I thought, "Is it a cultural belief system and perspective that's leading to these opposite polarities of result?"

It made me curious, and I started probing into the perception of loss or bereavement and grief. It led me to develop the grief resolution method I'll discuss in this chapter. It may shock you, because you may be accustomed to the mourning and gloom that surround death, but it's foolproof. Grieving can now be optional.

Grief: Not What It Seems

When a baby is born, most people will probably say, "Congratulations! That's wonderful." When somebody dies, they say to the survivors, "I'm so sorry for you." But when I went around and started talking to people who had just given birth and were dealing with deaths, I found an interesting fact.

As I've already emphasized, the mind has both conscious and unconscious parts. I found out that the women who had given birth were experiencing two things. One side was thinking, "I'm so glad I've had my baby!" But another part was thinking, "Oh, my God, what have I gotten myself into? This is overwhelming. For the next thirty years, I'm tied to this child." One side was more often socially expressed and conscious. While the other was more often socially repressed and unconscious, unless you asked the question that revealed it.

I then asked people who had recently lost grandparents, and they were crying about how this individual had died. But another part was thinking, "The challenge of having this slow death drag out is finally relieved."

In short, I found that at birth, there was both grief and relief, and at death, there was both grief and relief. Nobody seemed to want to talk about the other side. You're supposed to be happy when a baby's born: "Congratulations!" You're supposed to be sad when someone dies: "Oh, I'm sorry." Yet there were two sides. So that led me to probing what's creating that imbalance and why are people socially dividing and hiding half of their masks.

For thousands of years, people have been mourning and grieving over death, hiding the other side. I was fascinated. Why do some humans—and even some animals—do this, and can we have a way of overriding this response?

I'm certain that that's possible, and I'm going to show you how to do it. If you love to have grief go on and on, that's your business, but it does take its toll physiologically and psychologically. Staying in that state is not to your advantage. If it's prolonged, it can lead to health issues.

Let me state something that will shock you: *nobody has to live with grief ever again on planet Earth for more than three hours.* I can make that statement having demonstrated it clinically in thousands of clients or attendees.

There are two forms of grief. You've probably had people whom you perceived to be very supportive, and others that you perceived to challenge you. When someone supports your values, you tend to open up to them. When someone challenges your values, you tend to close down to them.

When you open up to someone, you're activating the amygdala. This part of the brain is activated in animals when they are seeking prey and avoiding predators. So when something supports your values, you register it like pleasureful prey. It's essential for your life, and you open up to it because you want to consume it. If something challenges your values, you see it as a kind of painful predator, which can kill you and eat you.

As a result, we naturally tend to seek prey and avoid predators. That's our animal nature, and that is the nature that gives rise to grief. Consequently, there are only two forms of grief. You can have the perception of loss of prey, which is food, or the perception of gain of a predator, which could eat you. One form of grief is the perception of loss of that which you are attracted to. When you're infatuated with somebody, you'll call them things like "honey," "sweetheart," "cupcake," "sweetie pie." You'll have language that is associated with the tongue, because when you're infatuated with something, you imagine it's sugary, and you want to open up to it.

When you are resentful to someone, instead of thinking of it as sweet, you regard them as bitter waste. You want to get rid of it. Every single-celled organism has processes to remove waste and toxins.

The lower subcortical amygdala or so-called animal brain is the brain center for seeking prey and avoiding predators. Grief is the perception of loss of what you seek and the gain of what you avoid. You can have grief over anything you're attracted to. If you get into a relationship that you like and your partner dumps you, you can have grief. The same is true if you lose money. Everything that you seek is registered in the primitive part of the brain as a kind of food. You can feel resentment and grief if you are deprived of it. Grief can have many sources: perceptions of loss of money, loved ones, respect, and influence in the world; loss of health, fitness, or beauty; loss of spiritual awareness. You can feel grief if you think you're losing your mind. Many people have addictions. If they're deprived of them, they show similar withdrawal symptoms of grief. Many symptoms of cold turkey withdrawal are actually from grief associated with the loss of the so-called pleasureful moments and brain content experienced when taking the drugs.

On the other side of the equation, you can have grief from the gain of anything that challenges you. If somebody sends you bills that you can't pay, it can cause grief. If an ex-spouse moves in next door remarried to someone half your age, that too could cause grief. Anything you don't want that comes near you can bring it on. In short, the loss of what you seek and the gain of what you avoid are the two sources of grief.

Taking thousands of people through this process, I've found that there's no conscious grief without unconscious relief. Again, they're like two poles of a magnet: they're inseparable.

Two Forms of Relief

There are also two forms of relief, and they're associated with the reverse of the examples I've just mentioned. Relief is the gain of that which you seek and the loss of that which you're trying to avoid. It's the reciprocal of grief. Let's say that you don't have money and you finally get some. That's a relief. Or you've lost your desired boyfriend or girlfriend, and they come back to you. Or you finally get food after having been hungry for a while. Or you have a business opportunity that gives you what you're looking for.

Relief also occurs from the loss of what you dislike or resent. If the bill collector says, "Forget it; don't worry about it; your bills are taken care of," you feel relief. If someone in the neighborhood who pushes your buttons moves away—oh, what a relief!

Relief is the perception of gain of that which you are seeking or the loss of that which you resent and want to avoid. For reasons that I've discussed in previous chapters, these two sides are linked. As I've also observed, when you're trying to live by other people's values rather than your own, you're more polarized in your perceptions, you tend to be subjective, and you create confirmation and disconfirmation biases in your perceptions. If you're living according to your highest values, you have a higher degree of objectivity, a more balanced view. Therefore you have more resilience and more adaptability.

Why does that apply to the grief process? When you see both sides of the deceased simultaneously, you have tremendous resilience. The more objective, resilient, and more balanced your view is, the more adaptable you are. People can come and go, and you're neither infatuated nor resentful. But if you're highly polarized, you're more vulnerable to split polarities and extremes of grief or relief.

In 2003, when the United States brought down Saddam Hussein, there was relief in America because we had a perception that he was a predator. But in some places in Iraq, there was grief, because those people saw him as a hero. The same for when Qasem Soleimani in Iran was killed by US air strikes. What was a relief of the loss of a villain in the US, was a grief of the loss of a hero in Iran.

Behavioral traits can be seen as either positive or negative. In fact, none of them are really either, but we make them so by our incomplete understanding and our limited viewpoint and biases. Moral projections of these positives and negatives as goods and bads are simply the result of a narrow mind. I've seen people be infatuated with a trait, then turn around and resent the same trait. I've also seen people resent a trait, then turn around and appreciate it. Traits are neither positive or negative, good or evil until we make them so. Absolute white and black views in morality are illusive and result in moral hypocrisies.

The majority of people live according to such white and black, prey and predator-like perceptions or animal-like behavior. They're living in a world of gain and losses, and they have highly emotional responses when people are born or die. I like to think that those who are more aware have a little less judgment and are more resilient to the inevitable balance of life and death, gain or loss. The masters of life live in a world of transformation. They're adaptable, they're resilient, and they're not trapped in extremes of attachment. They're able to move through things.

I've dealt with a woman who had her father say good-bye on the cell phone, then take a gun and shoot himself through the head in her living room. I've seen fresh, active, on the spot deaths. I've seen others who are still grieving twenty years after a death. Grief really has nothing to do with time, because you can grieve somebody who died decades ago, and dissolve the grief immediately or shortly after someone dies.

In the late 1990s, I was facilitating a workshop at Pfizer Pharmaceutical headquarters in New York, working with a group of Jewish men who had lived through and survived the Holocaust. They had seen their families die. They were still grieving forty-six years later.

I walked in with a picture of Adolf Hitler. I showed it to them, and their behavior was automatically withdrawn. Even though these people were in their sixties and seventies, they still had a marked emotional withdrawal response. We do not have any guarantee that time will dissolve emotional charges about events. We store them in our subconscious mind, and if we don't balance them, they can stay there for decades and keep running our lives. But if we balance these patterns, we're freed.

I've worked this method in both cases, and I've seen it work in each case and often. We work them live in front of the group in the Breakthrough Experience.

If I have somebody sitting in front of me that's grieving, I ask, "What specific trait, action, or inaction did you perceive this individual displaying or demonstrating that you admired most and now miss most since they have departed or become deceased?"

Many times the individual will come up with broad generalities and claim they are missing everything about them. Will they miss everything about the deceased though? "So you miss their dirty hair in the sink?" I ask. "You miss their smells? You miss their overeating? You miss them not paying bills? You miss their arguments? You miss their mess and clothes left on the floor? You miss their being later coming home for dinner?"

"Well, no, I don't miss those."

"So that means you don't miss everything." Nobody's going to miss the traits, actions, or inactions that they disliked about the deceased; they're only going to miss those they liked.

The individual will say, "Oh, my God. I realize that I'm only grieving the parts that I admired about them. I'm not grieving the parts that I disliked or even resented."

Even a long-term married couple has traits, actions, or inactions they like and dislike about each other. That's part of life. Yet after a death, people often want to paint a picture of the deceased as an amazing predominantly one-sided individual. They generate their own grief by creating their own one-sided fantasy. In order to help them, I enable them to confront that. I'm not here to make people feel some form of one-sided happiness. I'm here to help them get balanced and grounded so they can get on with their life and fully love the individual and be grateful for the time they were able to spend with both sides of them.

I ask, "What specific trait, action, or inaction do you believe you're missing or feeling the loss of?"

The grieving survivor will say something like, "Their support."

"What exactly is the action they took that supported you?"

"They encouraged me verbally."

"Great. Do you miss that?"

"Yes."

"What else do you miss? What else are you grieving the loss of?"

"Their timing and sense of humor. Their form of laughter."

"Good. What else are you missing?"

"Their advice. Their guidance."

"What else are you missing?"

"The time we spent together cooking. We would have amazing discussions about life. When we would eat and cook together, they'd listen to me, and I felt heard."

"Great. And you missed that?"

"Yeah."

"And what else?"

"Sometimes we used to go fishing together, and we would have discussions about our fishing technique."

"What else do you miss?"

"Our travels. We'd go traveling together."

"What else?"

I've discovered that with almost every death, you usually find about nine to eleven traits, actions, or inactions that the bereaved misses. The most I've seen is twenty-six; the least I've seen is four. Once the individual goes through and makes their most exhaustive list and they can't think of anything else and they go blank and they say, "That's it. That's all I miss. I'm grieving the loss of those things," we stop. They only list those traits, actions, inactions or qualities that supported the survivor's values; the survivor did not miss the others.

Once we have enumerated their complete list of missed behaviors, I tell the bereaved, "If anything else comes up during this process that you might remotely miss, please speak up and reveal it."

Next I ask, "The moment you found out that the deceased passed away and they're no longer there to provide those behaviors, who from that moment until now has emerged and increased their behaviors to compensate?"

At first they say, "Nobody."

"Look again."

"I'd never thought about it."

"Look carefully. The moment this individual passed, who emerged in your life to take on those behaviors, those traits?"

All of a sudden, they say, "That's interesting. When my wife died, her sister started to do some of those behaviors. She came around and started interacting with me and doing three or four of those behaviors."

"Great. Who else?"

"Now that I think about it, my daughter's taken on some of that role."

"Who else?"

"There's a lady at work that's kind of nurturing me."

I keep asking. I don't want them to make up anything. I just want them to look, and to their surprise they discover that what they thought they had missed surfaced in one or many other people. It could occur in males or females. It could occur in self or other. You could actually take on a trait of the departed or deceased.

I had a gentleman whose twelve-year-old boy passed away. He missed putting Velcro shoes on his son's feet, because he had Down syndrome, and he couldn't do that himself.

"So the moment he passed away, who started doing that?"

"I don't know. I can't think of anyone."

"My certainty exceeds your doubt. Take a look again."

The gentleman's wife was there, and all of a sudden, she spoke up and said, "Honey, isn't it interesting? You never had a Velcro pair of shoes until he died. You've been playing soccer now as he used to play."

"You're right. I have. I didn't even think about it."

The individual could be self or other, male or female, one or many, close or distant. I've been doing this process since 1984, and I've yet to find somebody who can't answer that question if I hold them accountable to keep looking and digging. All of a sudden, they say, "I can't believe it. I'm now surrounded by people that do that. A lot of them have increased doing that, even though they didn't even notice it before."

"Exactly. And you may have taken on some behaviors yourself."

My wife passed away many years ago. Prior to that, she had been writing for twenty-seven magazines in different parts of the world. The moment she passed away, for some reason, magazines came out of the woodwork for me. I've written for, or been interviewed for, about 1,500 magazines around the world. I took on part of that role. I also hung out with different people who wrote for magazines and publishing and related actions.

By the way, I've asked a lot of people this: "Do you really want the people you care about to grieve, or do you want them to get on with their life and live it to the fullest?" I've yet to have anybody look me straight in the eye and say, "I want the people I care about to grieve upon my passing or departure." When people die, they want their survivors to have a great life and fulfillment. So when we're grieving, we can ask ourselves whether it has anything to do with the one who died or whether it has something do with our own processing, internal conflicts, biased views of the deceased and socially indoctrinated belief systems.

When my wife passed away, I did this method or exercise and passed through her transition very beautifully and smoothly. In fact, I helped many people who were distraught about her death dissolve their grief. They were puzzled: Why was I was able to feel love for and the presence of the deceased instead of feeling grief and loss?

When you truly and fully love both sides of someone, you feel their presence. I've proven that in the Breakthrough Experience with over 100,000 people. But when you're infatuated or resentful and you have split emotions about people, you can have these senses of grief and relief.

Let's go back to the process. I go through and write in the initials of the people who do what the deceased used to do until the list is quantitatively equal. And I say, "Are you now certain that these newly emerged people have compensated for 100 percent of the deceased's admired and now missed behavior?"

If the survivor says, "Not quite," I ask them to keep looking again and again until they say, "Oh yeah, I forgot about this individual. At work this has happened," and so on. They realize that it is quantitatively balanced. It's shocking to people, because they have not been exposed to that question or even thought about it before. It's not taught anywhere. And they are not allowed to make anything up or guess. They are only allowed to write answers they are certain about.

It's a discovery that I made studying physics. There's the law of conservation of energy, information, and matter: it's just changing forms. I believe life is the same way. As Buckminster Fuller said, "There's no death in the scenario of the universe: only transformation."

I've presented the Breakthrough Experience over 1,560 times, with an average of seventy-plus people each time. Thousands of people have gone through this experience, and I've trained thousands of facilitators who have gone out and used this grief dissolving method repeatedly. I've used it after the Ishinomaki earthquake in Japan in 2011, as well as the more recent Fukushima earthquake in 2016. I did it after the 2011 earthquake in Christchurch, New Zealand. I've been using this method on serious, real-life issues for a long period of time now, and it works. This is a very powerful message. It can change the way you perceive death. In 2018 a research pilot study was conducted at Keio University in Japan and the researchers were astonished at the significance of the 100 percent lasting results.

Grieving the Infatuations

In the next step of this process, I deal with what the grieving individual was originally admiring or infatuated with in the departed or deceased, because you only grieve the loss of those traits, actions or inactions, that you like or admire. The individual is grieving because they perceive more benefits than drawbacks, more positives than negatives, more support than challenge in those selected behaviors of the deceased. If they saw more drawbacks than benefits, there would be relief, not grief.

I neutralize the perceived benefits by finding the other side. If the individual is choosing to not see the downsides of a trait, that's their own unconscious blindness. I'm convinced that our polarized emotions are the result of incomplete awareness, but love sees both sides. When people truly finish this method, there's love, presence, and gratitude. If they have not, there's still a polarized emotion and I keep working.

I don't consider true unconditional love and gratitude as polarized emotions. I believe that they're the synthesis and synchronicity of any pair of complementary opposite, polarized emotions. Emotions reflect an imbalanced state. When we balance them, we have a deepest and truest form of, "Thank you, I love you." By the way, that's the true essence of our existence. If you had only twenty-four hours to live, what would you do? You would go to the people you care about and say, "Thank you, I love you."

In any event, if the grieving individual is consciously fixated on the upsides of the individual, they will be grieving the "loss" of these. And they are unconscious of downsides of the individual's up-sided behaviors. So, I ask, "What was the drawback of that individual's upsided behavior when they were alive; what were their downsides when they displayed them?" I do not want them to state any assumed, made up, or speculative answers, only truly perceived drawbacks, downsides, negatives, or challenging aspects of the admired behaviors they assumed had no downsides.

At first they usually say, "I can't think of any; I don't know. There aren't any."

"No," I say, "every trait has two sides. So what were the downsides?"

To their surprise, when they start digging, the unconscious comes forward, and memories of some of the negatives and downsides start surfacing. Like I just mentioned, I don't want anything that's made up; I don't want anything that the individual is not certain about. I want them to dig until they find the other side of the equation concerning the admired behavior, because traits are neutral until somebody with a narrow mind labels them as either good or bad, positive or negative.

By the way, if something really were a bad trait, it would have gone extinct, because it wouldn't be serving anything. But these traits have lasted for thousands of years, so they do serve us. Our subjectively biased ignorance is what labels them either good or bad. The truth is, they're both or neither, depending on how you look at them situationally and how they relate to the artificial context you have projecting on to it.

So I ask them, "What's the drawback of that specific trait, action, or inaction that they admired?" I start listing all the drawbacks. I keep them answering that question until the number of drawbacks and disadvantages is perfectly balanced with the benefits and advantages.

Sometimes people say, "I miss their guidance."

I ask, "What were the downsides or drawbacks of their guidance?"

"I can't think of any."

"Let's look again."

All of a sudden the individual says, "They actually guided me foolishly on a stock deal, and I lost money."

"What else?"

"They guided me on how to handle my kids, and now that I think about it, that wasn't the wisest way to do it."

Again, I continue this process until the drawbacks equal the benefits. I say, "Are you now certain that there are just as many drawbacks as benefits to each of the previously admired behaviors listed?" If there's even the slightest hesitation, I keep them going until there is certainty.

Already the grieving individual is starting to have a shift. Then I go over to each of the new people who are now displaying or demonstrating that specific trait, action, or inaction for that individual and ask, "What's the benefit and advantages of these people coming on board and playing that role or displaying and demonstrating the behavior?"

They say, "The advice is more up-to-date, more current, more in line with what I really want with my current highest values. I'm not feeling obligated to have to satisfy what this individual wants from their guidance. Advice is more diverse. I'm getting more varieties of opinions. It allows me to make decisions myself. I'm not dependent. I'm more empowered."

As I write in the benefits of those who are now providing those specific traits or behaviors, to their surprise, the individual realizes that the new forms are very much in line with what they highly value at this moment. It's almost as if they're now realizing that maybe this death is serving a higher purpose: "I'm not as attached to the old or previous individual's way. I'm now moving forward again."

Once the benefits and drawbacks are completely balanced, I ask, "Are you grieving the loss of this individual now?"

They'll say, "No."

You won't and can't grieve the loss of someone that's honestly and perfectly balanced perceptually. I keep doing that all the way down the list. On average, this could take anywhere from forty-five minutes to the highest I've seen, which is three hours. That's why I say nobody has to grieve more than three hours on planet Earth again. When you complete the method, you will feel love and gratitude for them and for their contribution to your life and their presence.

Once I'm done and we've checked off these items, the individual's face is different. Their physiology is different. Their brain chemistry has changed, because grief is a result of an imbalanced perspective.

I challenge the notion, prevalent in pharmaceutics and psychiatry, that depression and grief are caused by biochemical imbalances. I've got people who were clinically depressed and changed them in less than three hours. I'll bet if they went back, they would find that their brain chemistry changed. The chemistry is not the cause; it is more often the correlated effect. I'm amazed at how people are told that they've got a biochemical imbalance or that it could take years to get over grief. That's because of incompetence and ignorance—not knowing how the brain works and not knowing how to help people efficiently.

If I'm facilitating this method in front of a group, I'll ask the grieving individual who has been selected by the group to, "Look around the room. Who here represents or reminds you of the individual that you just previously grieved the loss of?" They look around the room, and there'll be somebody who resembles or reminds them of the deceased individual that they did the method on. I'll ask this surrogate individual to come up and sit across from the subject in a chair, and I'll hand them tissues, because what they're about to do will bring up a tear. Not a tear of sorrow or of grief—a tear of love and gratitude.

I'll get these two people very close to each other and I'll ask, "What's in your heart that you want to share with the individual who is deceased or departed now?"

They'll start to speak, and they'll both go into a sort of trance state; they won't notice the rest of the room. The one who has been grieving will say what they feel naturally grateful for from their heart, and the other individual will reply as if they actually were the one who is deceased or departed. The two of them will converse in a warm and heart opening, seemingly telepathic manner. It's mind-blowing to see this in action. When they're finished, they'll hug each other spontaneously, and they'll have tears of gratitude and love. They will both feel as if the deceased or departed individual is actually present.

Afterward, when they come back from their temporary trance state, I'll hold up a microphone to the individual so the whole room can hear. I'll say, "Right now, are you grieving the loss of this individual?"

"No."

"Do you feel their presence?"

"Yes."

"Do you have love and appreciation for them?"

"Yes."

"There's no grief is there?"

"No."

"Try to show grief. Try to access grief."

"I can't."

"Try, try as hard as you can. Try to find if you can get grief."

"It's not there."

No, because it's not possible to have grief unless you have an imbalanced perspective.

Resistance and Strategies

Nevertheless, I've seen a few people who have resisted doing the method because they had a hidden agenda and strategy in mind. Let me give you an example. I had a lady who had married into a very wealthy family, but the husband's parents, particularly his mother, did not want her son to be married to her. The parents told him, "She's beneath you. You deserve a higher quality breed of woman than this." But he dated and soon impregnated her, and he felt partly morally trapped. That's how he and his family, especially the mother, perceived it. The son felt obligated to take on care of the child and married the lady against his parents' wishes.

When the child, a son, turned sixteen, he started dating a girl who liked some interesting behaviors. They ended up doing a sexual act in which he choked and hanged himself and died.

The lady was referred to me because she was demonstrating prolonged grief syndrome for over a year, and so I worked with her privately. She was strangely resisting answering the questions encompassed within the Demartini Method, and I finally said, "There appears to be a distinct motive here for not digging in and uncovering the answers. What's your hidden agenda or motive for such a resistance?"

The woman realized that if she didn't have a child and she didn't grieve, there's no reason the family would allow her husband to stay in her life. He could move on, and she didn't want to lose the lifestyle and the opportunities that he provided. As long as she was grieving, the man wasn't going anywhere and the parents would not pressure him to move on. So she was, partly consciously and partly unconsciously, using grief to keep the family dynamic going and make sure she had an income, prestige, and security. It's amazing how strategic we are at times to remain secure.

During this lengthier session, as I was applying the method, it become essential to dissolve her infatuation with what the man and the family provided and bring it into balance. I spent about four hours in total with her, which is way longer than most cases. Once we cleared those elements concerning the position of the parents versus herself, and I leveled the playing field, the grief was done. Dealing with the actual grief probably took about forty-five minutes to an hour, but a lot of work was required to deal with the security issues that were blocking her from doing the method.

In the end, the woman didn't have grief. She actually confessed that her son was doing drugs. He was bringing drugs in the house, and he was causing problems and potentially legal concerns. "We were afraid we were going to get in trouble and we were going to have legal bills and other challenges of this nature. He wasn't regularly going to school. He was out of control."

Suddenly, the unrevealed aspects of her son that she resented came to the surface. Part of her was relieved that he had passed away, even though she was pretending to show grief. She had mixed feelings which was at least more truthful.

Let me state something that's going to shock you: the greater the grief, the more hidden the relief. They're pairs of opposites. They're entangled. So don't be fooled by outer appearances and the conscious show. Dig deep. That's why this grief resolution method is very valuable: it helps integrate people, gives them some objective, and puts them in touch with reason and returns them to a balanced state of gratitude and love. Ralph Waldo Emerson asked, why, instead of crying with sympathy for people, don't we get them back in touch with reality?

This method gets the individual in touch with what they truthfully and actually perceived, which contains both their conscious and unconscious sides now fully conscious. When they're done, they give me a hug and say, "Thank you. I'm freed. I'm not grieving. I feel the presence of the one I love. I love this individual. I'm not infatuated or resentful. I'm just feeling their presence, and it's heart opening."

Usually when I do the method at a seminar, not only are the two people in tears of gratitude, but so is the whole room. Many of those present who have also experienced deaths or losses are sitting, processing, and seeing their own lives. We have ripple effects throughout the seminar program.

This method works. Once, around 1988, I flew out to San Diego and had a car service take me up the beaches to Del Mar. I was intending to present my method to a famous psychologist there, who refused my offer and pooh-poohed it, saying, "If there was something like what you are describing, I would know about it." He wasn't interested in hearing what I had to share. I was a bit shocked, but simply turned around and flew back to Texas and just assumed either I did not present it to him in a manner that met his values or he was just not interested in some alternative method at that moment.

Ironically, in 2007 I was presenting the Breakthrough Experience in Maui, and lo and behold, the same gentleman—without even realizing that I was the same guy that had been to his office—came to my seminar. He had lost his wife. He came up on stage, and I did the process with him and cleared his grief. By some improbable coincidence he was the individual selected by the group to be the case that I demonstrate the method on since he was well known and his wife had recently passed. After going through the entire method over nearly two hours and completing the process with a heart-opening surrogate experience, he said, "That was amazing. I could swear my wife was just here with me just a moment ago and now I'm not grieving."

I couldn't help myself but I then stated, "by the way, do you remember me from 1988?"

"No."

"I'm the guy who tried to present this method to you back then." "Oh, my God! I remember that now. I was a cocky son of a gun and pushed you right out of my office."

"You were, but I'm grateful that the universe brought us back together again, because now you know."

He then intentionally promoted my work and told people about it. I don't know of anybody who's gone through this work that hasn't told people about it, because there's no reason for someone to be grieving. It's absolutely unnecessary.

The Relief Side

Before a first baby is born, the mother is quite often a bit elated: "Oh, I'm going to be so happy when I have a baby." When the baby comes, she can be a bit naïve and have an unrealistic expectation—a fantasy—and as a result, she can become depressed after the birth. The prepartum reds can result in postpartum blues. I've rarely seen a depressed mom who didn't have a fantasy prior to the baby's arrival. Again, depression is a comparison of current reality to a fantasy that you're holding on to. Many times when mothers have a baby, they're envisioning a bit of a one-sided fantasy, "There are going to be more benefits than drawbacks." But like everything else, pregnancy and mothering has both sides.

When a baby is born, I ask, "What specific traits, actions, or inactions in the new baby do you think you've gained?"

"I got my physical baby to hold and cuddle. I've got someone I love desiring to be nurtured. I have somebody with beautiful eyes looking up at me. I have somebody suckling on my breasts and milk. I have somebody needing my assistance and love. I have somebody that requires my assistance in being dressed and clothed."

I write down the admired behaviors that they think they've gained when the baby has been born. Again, it's usually nine to ten items on average, sometimes more. I think eighteen is about the most I've seen on this one, and the least I've seen is about six.

Then I ask, "Prior to that birth, who was providing those specific traits or behaviors?" I compile the names of the people who provided the same or similar traits in some form. Most of the time, it's the husband. The husband was nurturing, but now that the baby's there, the husband and wife are more distant. They don't have the time for each other, because she's dedicating it to the baby. The husband was being fed and clothed and had intimacy. All of a sudden, that's been partly withdrawn. It's like: "OK, the donor has supplied the sperm. Now I need to focus on the child." It's not uncommon. Some women pay a price if they don't know how to balance that, because the husband ends up feeling neglected.

Sometimes there's a lot of infatuation with certain traits displayed by the baby at first. If there is, I request the mother to find the one or many individuals who displayed or provided the traits before. All of a sudden, the mother realizes she didn't gain anything; she merely changed the forms. Remember, the masters live in a world of transformation; the masses live in the illusions of gain and loss.

Then I ask, "What are the drawbacks of the new form?"

"I'm not going to have as much sleep at night, and when I look in those eyes, sometimes the baby is crying and screaming at me. Sometimes I don't want to look at them, because the baby is screaming."

You start adding it up, you see the drawbacks, and you find the benefits of the old form. When you do, you balance them until they're qualitatively and quantitatively equal.

When the mother does this, she becomes more grounded and understanding of the new family dynamic. They're not infatuated or resentful about the child. They feel love and presence for the child and the husband. The child can feel it and shows it in its behavior, because the moment you have a true presence and true love, the child calms down. Many of the child's emotional symptoms have a lot to do with the infatuations and resentments that are stored in the unconscious portions of the minds of the mom and dad. Once those are balanced, the child can pick it up. They're more poised, and their development is less volatile, with fewer emotional swings. Children can balance out and defuse family tensions, judgments, and conflicts.

The second these poles are balanced, you realize that there was not a gain or a loss, but there was a transformation. The transformation's not better or worse, so there's no moral issue here. You just honor the transformation by being unattached and having the ability to resiliently adapt to a changing environment, because the truth is, our world is changing every moment of every day. By neutralizing the illusion of loss or gain, you become more adaptable and resilient.

Grieving $750 Million

This tool is not limited to strictly life and death. You could have a loss of money. I had a gentleman who was a hedge fund manager that perceived that he had lost $750 million. We did this exercise in forty-eight minutes and cleared his grief. He stacked up everything that he thought he'd lost, put a dollar value on it, and found out that the new form that had come into his life was equivalent to that dollar value. What was the benefit of the new form; what was the drawback of the old form?

The man realized that his partner in the hedge fund had been doing things that were illegal. And his partner took this gentleman's money and disappeared offshore. The following day the man found out his bank and investment accounts were cleaned out to the tune of $750 million. Until he came to the Breakthrough Experience, he was extremely bitter and angry, and had occasional heart issues and palpitations whenever he thought about the event. He wanted to kill the other guy.

Then I asked, "So what did you gain from this apparent loss? You don't lose anything without gaining. It's a transformation."

The man started laughing. He said, "I got rid of a wife that was a gold digger. She was using me for money and wasn't really interested in me. I got rid of her without having to pay a big price, because I'd been wanting to divorce her for about five years. When my partner took the money, she just left, and I didn't have anything. The divorce was quick and uncontested. I would have had to give her $360 million, and I didn't feel she was worth it, so I just endured the unfulfilling marriage. I also got my health back, because I had been working so much and had significant hypertension. Since this happened, I've been working out and trying to get back in shape again. I've attracted somebody in my life that actually wants me for who I am. It's not about my money, because I've got no money.

"When my partner took the money, the clients weren't angry at me; they were angry at my partner, because I'd gotten taken too. I got the clients, and I got the legal team. Now that I see it, I have the ability to rebuild my entire company, and this guy's probably going to go to prison. If he hadn't stolen the money, I might be in prison today because of some of the things he was doing with our client's money.

"This is the best day of my life. I now realize that his taking $750 million was a gift." He was grateful for the man and for what happened.

It doesn't matter if you've lost money. It doesn't matter if you've lost an arm or an eye. It doesn't matter what the loss is; this method works because it's based on the perception of what supports or challenges your values. Once you understand that, you can neutralize any gain that you got excited about, and then feel your loss. I have been fortunate to help many individuals with a wild variety of apparent losses.

Some people ask, why would you want to neutralize excitement? Isn't it good to be excited? No, not necessarily. It too has two sides. Because if you become infatuated with a manic-producing fantasy, you set yourself up for depression as soon as you perceive it to be lost. You're setting yourself up for the next loss by getting attached to the fantasy form. Having excitement means that you are temporarily blind to the downsides.

If you're highly infatuated with somebody, you're going to fear their loss. If you are more balanced and love somebody, you're going to feel their presence. The Demartini Method helps people go back and return to thankfulness and love and realize the hidden order and conserved balance of the world around us. It helps them appreciate and be adaptable and resilient no matter what happens. It allows them to see from an objective rather than a subjective view, which helps them live in their executive center, not their amygdala. It helps them understand that we're not stuck with only the animal behavior inside us; we can have command over it. We can let it rule our lives and be a victim of its history, or we can overrule it and be a master of our destiny.

It is possible that the individual may think of two or three things later that hadn't occurred to them during the process. I've seen this a couple of times over the years. If so, simply repeat the four-step process on those specific behaviors you initially overlooked and once again dissolve their incomplete and imbalanced perceptions.

The Loss of a Grandmother

I was in Prince Edward Island, in Canada, because a psychologist asked me to come and present the Demartini Method. They brought in the psychology departments from their own university and two others nearby.

Some people were wanting to debate and initially trying to rebut my method, saying, "Oh, no, you can't do that. It is important to let people grieve. It's natural. It's healthy."

I said, "We can dilly-dally all day long and play mental games. Why don't I just do the process? Is there anybody here who's grieving?"

A number of hands went up. In the end, we picked a young woman who had perceived that she had lost her grandmother two days earlier. The grandmother raised this young woman as if she was her biological mother, and the young woman was obviously perceiving loss and feeling grief. She had tears and had difficulty speaking, with a quivering mouth.

I went through the process with her in front of the whole group in a full amphitheater. It took an hour and fifteen minutes. At the end, the young woman had gratitude, presence, and love.

I said, "Now try your best to see if you can access grief."

"I can't." She had a different look on her face. She had a feeling of poise.

Some people said, "How long is that going to last?"

I said, "To those who believe, no proof is necessary. To those who don't, no proof is possible. I can waste my time debating, but why don't you follow up with this girl a week, a month, a year from now, and make your own decisions? She's a human being. She can tell you what she's experiencing."

Afterword

The Journey of Resilience

We've taken a long journey in this book. We've seen a lot about what resilience is and how we can strengthen it.

We've learned that the single most important way to strengthen your resilience is to live according to your own highest values—not your parents', not your spouse's or partner's, not society's. When we live according to our highest values, we function in a higher part of the brain, which knows how to govern difficult situations and regain equilibrium.

We've seen how you can undo your own unconscious agendas, which are often the greatest hindrances to vitality, progress, and attainment of the goals you most value. We've even seen how living in a state of congruence (as I call it) can reshape and restore the nervous system.

Resilience, as we've seen, has a great deal to do with facing and overcoming life's distracting fantasies and hard knocks. Sometimes what seem to be the greatest lifts or blows and fortunes or misfortunes contain within them the seeds of our greatest and most authentic blessings. We can even use the symptoms of either form or polarity of illness to reorient ourselves toward wholeness and balance.

The key to overcoming depression, grief, and anxiety is learning about the inherent balance of human psychology and physiology, the homeostasis governing life: there are no positives without negatives, no negatives without positives. Depression and anxiety are often the result of focusing on one aspect without acknowledging the other.

There are simple and specific methods for overcoming these illusive difficulties and enhancing resilience—sometimes generating what sometimes appears to be miraculous results. I promise you, these are tools that you can use.

By the way, for those of you who would love to experience the Demartini Method live and observe its impact and power, please consider joining me at the Breakthrough Experience, or if you would love to add the method to your current tool kit, I have the Demartini Method Training Program for anyone who would love to learn how to do exactly this. If you're a counselor, coach, therapist, or anybody else who is helping people dealing with infatuation, resentment, pride, shame, loss, grief, or bereavement, please consider taking the training program, because you then help me help other people using it. To find out more, please visit my website: drdemartini.com.

About the Author

Dr. John Demartini is a human behavioral specialist and founder of the Demartini Institute, a private research and education institute dedicated to activating self-mastery, leadership, and greater human potential. He is an international best-selling author and business consultant, working with CEOs of Fortune 500 companies, celebrities, and sports personalities. Globally, he's worked with individuals and groups across many markets, including entrepreneurs, financiers, psychologists, teachers, and young adults, assisting and guiding them to greater levels of achievement, fulfillment, and empowerment in many areas of their lives.

For more information about Dr. John Demartini, his live events, and range of products, contact the Demartini Institute at info@drdemartini.com. To view his website, visit drdemartini.com.